THE TOOLS

THE
TOOLS

5 TOOLS TO
HELP YOU FIND
COURAGE, CREATIVITY,
AND WILLPOWER—
AND INSPIRE YOU
TO LIVE LIFE
IN FORWARD MOTION

**Phil Stutz
and
Barry Michels**

Random House
New York

2013 Trade Paperback Edition

Published in the United States by Random House, an imprint and
division of Penguin Random House LLC, New York.

RANDOM HOUSE and the HOUSE colophon are registered
trademarks of Penguin Random House LLC.

Originally published in hardcover in the United States by Spiegel &
Grau, an imprint of Random House, a division of Penguin Random
House LLC, in Canada by Random House Canada, Toronto, and in the
United Kingdom by Vermilion, a part of Ebury Publishing, a division
of the Random House Group Ltd., London, in 2012.

LIBRARY OF CONGRESS CATALOGING-IN-PUBLICATION DATA

Stutz, Phil.
The tools: 5 tools to help you find courage, creativity, and
willpower—and inspire you to live life in forward motion / Phil Stutz,
Barry Michels.
p.   cm.
ISBN 978-0-8129-8304-3
eBook ISBN 978-0-679-64445-3
1. Self-actualization (Psychology) 2. Change (Psychology) I. Stutz,
Phil. II. Title.
BF637.S4M523 2012   158—dc23   2011044717

Printed in the United States of America on acid-free paper

randomhousebooks.com

30 29 28 27 26 25 24 23

Book design by Donna Sinisgalli

To Lucy Quvus, who never let me give up.

—PHIL STUTZ

To my sister Debra, a spiritual warrior
of the highest order, who taught me to live
with grace, courage, and love.

—BARRY MICHELS

Sweet are the uses of adversity,

Which like the toad, ugly and venomous,

Wears yet a precious jewel in his head.

—WILLIAM SHAKESPEARE,

AS YOU LIKE IT

The things which hurt, instruct.

—BENJAMIN FRANKLIN

CONTENTS

THE TOOLS

Revelation of a New Way

ROBERTA WAS A NEW PSYCHOTHERAPY PATIENT who made me feel completely ineffective within fifteen minutes of meeting her. She had come to me with a very specific goal: she wanted to stop obsessing about the idea that her boyfriend was cheating on her. "I go through his messages, grill him with questions; sometimes I even drive by his place to spy on him. I never find anything but I can't stop myself." I thought her problem was easily explained by the fact that her father had abruptly deserted the family when she was a child. Even now, in her mid-twenties, she was still terrified of abandonment. But before we could delve into that issue more deeply, she looked me in the eye and demanded, "Tell me how I can stop obsessing. Don't waste my time and money on *why* I'm insecure—I already know."

If Roberta came to see me today, I'd be thrilled that she knew exactly what she wanted, and I'd know exactly how to help her. But my meeting with her took place twenty-five years ago when I was a new psychotherapist. I felt the directness of her request shoot through me like an arrow. I had no response.

I didn't blame myself. I had just spent two years devouring every current theory of psychotherapeutic practice. But the more information I digested, the more unsatisfied I became. The theories felt removed from the actual experience someone would have when he or she was in trouble and needed help. I felt in my gut that I hadn't been taught a way to respond directly to what a patient like Roberta was asking for.

I wondered, Maybe I can't pick up this ability from a book; maybe it can be learned only in face-to-face consultation with someone who'd been in the trenches. I had developed close ties to two of my supervisors—not only did they know me well, but they had many decades of clinical experience. Surely, they must have developed some way to meet these requests.

I described Roberta's demand to them. Their response confirmed my worst fears. They had no solution. Worse, what seemed to me like a reasonable request, they saw as part of her problem. They used a lot of clinical terms: Roberta was "impulsive," "resistant," and "craved immediate gratification." If I tried to meet her immediate needs, they warned me, she would actually become more demanding.

Unanimously, they advised me to guide her back to her childhood—there we would find what caused the obsession in the first place. I told them she already knew why she was obsessed. Their answer was that her father's abandonment couldn't be the *real* reason. "You have to go even *deeper* into her childhood." I was fed up with this runaround: I'd heard it before—every time a patient made a direct request, the therapist would turn it back on the patient and tell him or her to "go deeper." It was a shell game they used to hide the truth: when it came to immediate help, these therapists had very little to give to their patients. Not only was I disappointed, I had the sinking feeling that my supervisors were speaking for the entire psychotherapeutic profession—certainly I'd never heard anyone say anything else. I didn't know where to turn.

Then I got lucky. A friend told me he'd met a psychiatrist who didn't accept the system any more than I did. "This guy actually answers your questions—and I guarantee you've never heard these answers before." He was giving a series of seminars, and I decided to go to the next one. That was where I met Dr. Phil Stutz, the coauthor of this book.

That seminar changed my practice—and my life.

Everything about the way Phil thought seemed completely new. More important, in my gut it felt like the truth. He was the first psychotherapist I'd met whose focus was on the solution, not the problem. He was absolutely confident that human beings possessed untapped forces that allowed them to solve their own problems. In fact, his view of problems was the opposite of what I'd been taught. He didn't see them as handicapping the patient; he saw them as opportunities to enter this world of untapped potential.

I was skeptical at first. I'd heard about turning problems into opportunities before, but no one had ever explained exactly how to do this. Phil made it clear and concrete. You had to tap into hidden resources by means of certain powerful but simple techniques that anyone could use.

He called these techniques "tools."

I walked out of that seminar so excited, I felt like I could fly. It wasn't just that there were actual tools that could help people; it was something about Phil's attitude. He was laying himself, his theories, and his tools out in the open. He didn't demand that we accept what he was telling us; the only thing he insisted on was that we actually use his tools and come to our own conclusions about what they could do. He almost dared us to prove him wrong. He struck me as very brave or mad—possibly both. But in any case, the effect on me was catalyzing, like bursting out into the fresh air after the suffocating dogma of my more traditional colleagues. I saw even more clearly how much they hid behind an impenetrable wall of convoluted ideas, none of which they felt the need to test or experience for themselves.

I had learned only one tool at the seminar, but as soon as I left, I practiced it religiously. I couldn't wait to give it to Roberta. I was sure it would help her more than delving deeper into her past. In our next session, I said, "Here's something you can do the moment you start to obsess," and I gave her the tool (I'll present it later). To my amazement, she seized on it and started using it immediately. More amazingly, it helped. My colleagues had been wrong. Giving Roberta something that provided immediate help didn't make her more demanding and immature; it inspired her to become an active, enthusiastic participant in her own therapy.

I'd gone from feeling useless to having a very positive impact on someone in a very short time. I found myself hungering for more—more information, more tools; a deeper understanding of how they worked. Was this just a grab bag of different techniques, or was it what I suspected—a whole new way of looking at human beings?

In an effort to get answers, I began to corner Phil at the end of each seminar and squeeze as much information as I could out of him. He was always cooperative—he seemed to like answering questions—but each answer led to another question. I felt I'd hit the mother lode of information, and I wanted to take home as much of it as possible. I was insatiable.

Which brought up another issue. What I was learning from Phil was so powerful that I wanted it to be the core of my work with patients. But there was no training program to apply to, no academic hurdles to jump over. That was stuff I was good at, but he seemed to have no interest in it, which made me feel insecure. How could I qualify to be trained? Would he even think of me as a candidate? Was I turning him off with my questions?

Not too long after I began giving the seminars, this intense young guy named Barry Michels began to show up. With some hesitation, he identified himself as a therapist, although, given the detailed way he questioned me, he sounded more like a lawyer. Whatever he was, he was really smart.

But that's not why I answered his questions. I've never been impressed by intellect or credentials. What caught my attention was how enthusiastic he was; how he'd go home and use the tools himself. I didn't know if I was imagining it, but I felt as though he'd been looking for something for a long time and had finally found it.

Then he asked me a question I'd never been asked before.

"I was wondering. . . . Who taught you this stuff . . . the tools and everything? My training program didn't touch on anything remotely like it."

"No one taught me."

"You mean you came up with this yourself?"

I hesitated. "Yeah . . . well, not exactly."

I didn't know if I should tell him how I really got the information. But he seemed open-minded, so I decided to give it a try. It was a somewhat unusual story, that began with the very first patients I treated, and one in particular.

Tony was a young surgical resident at the hospital where I was a resident in psychiatry. Unlike a lot of the other surgeons, he wasn't arrogant, in fact when I first saw him, cowering near the door of my office, he looked like a trapped rat. When I asked him what was wrong, he answered, "I'm afraid of a test I have to take." He was shaking like the test was in ten minutes; but it wasn't scheduled for another six months. All tests scared him—and this one was a big one. It was his board-certification exam in surgery.

I interpreted his history the way I'd been trained to. His father had made a fortune in dry cleaning but was a college dropout with deep feelings of inferiority. On the surface, he wanted his son to become a famous surgeon to gain a vicarious sense of success. But underneath, he was so insecure that he was threatened by the idea of his son surpassing him. Tony was unconsciously terrified to succeed for this reason: his father would see him as a rival and retaliate. Failing his exams was his way of keeping himself safe. At least that was what I'd been trained to believe.

When I gave this interpretation to Tony, he was skeptical. "That sounds like something out of a textbook. My father has never pushed me to do anything for his sake. I can't blame my problem on him." Still, it seemed to help at first; he looked and felt better. But as the day of the test drew closer, his anxiety returned. He wanted to postpone the exam. I assured him this was just his unconscious fear of his father. All he had to do was keep talking about it, and it would go away again. This was the traditional, time-tested approach to his problem. I was so confident that I guaranteed he'd pass his test.

I was wrong. He failed miserably.

We had one last session after that. He still looked like a trapped rat, but this time an angry trapped rat. His words echoed in my ears. "You didn't give me a real way to conquer fear. Talking about my father every time was like fighting a gorilla with a water pistol. You failed me."

My experience with Tony opened my eyes. I realized how helpless patients could feel facing a problem by themselves. What they needed were solutions that would give them the power to fight back. Theories and explanations couldn't give that kind of power; they needed *forces* they could feel.

I had a series of other, less spectacular failures. In each case, a patient was in some state of suffering: depression, panic, obsessional rage, etc. They pleaded with me for a way to make their pain go away. I had no idea how to help them.

I was experienced at dealing with failure. I was addicted to basketball growing up and played with kids bigger and better than I was. (Actually, almost everybody was bigger than I was.) If I performed badly at basketball, I just practiced more. This was different. Once I lost faith in the way I'd been taught to do therapy, there was nothing to practice. It was as though someone took the ball away.

My supervisors were sincere and dedicated, but they attributed my doubts to inexperience. They told me most young therapists doubt themselves, but as time passes, they learn that therapy can only do so much. By accepting its limitations, they don't feel as bad about themselves.

But those limitations were unacceptable to me.

I wouldn't be satisfied until I could offer patients what they asked for: a way to help themselves now. I decided I would find a way to do this no matter where it took me. Looking back, I realize that this was the next step on a path that had started when I was a child.

When I was nine, my three-year-old brother died of a rare cancer. My parents, who had limited emotional resources, never recovered. A cloud of doom hung over them. This tragedy changed my role in the family. Their hope for the future became focused on me—as if I had a special power to make the doom go away. Each evening my father would come home from work, sit in his rocking chair, and worry.

He didn't do it quietly.

I'd sit on the floor next to his chair, and he'd warn me that his business might go bankrupt any day (he called it "going busted"). He'd ask me stuff like "Could you make do with only one pair of pants?" Or "What if we all had to live in one room?" None of his fears were realistic; they were as close as he could come to admitting his terror that death would visit us again. Over the next few years, I realized my job was to reassure him. In effect, I became my father's shrink.

I was twelve years old.

Not that I thought about it that way. I didn't think at all. I was moved by an instinctive fear that if I didn't accept this role, doom would overwhelm us. As unrealistic as that fear was, it felt absolutely real at the time. Being under that kind of pressure as a kid gave me strength when I grew up and got real patients. Unlike many of my peers, I wasn't intimidated by their demands. I'd been in that role for almost twenty years.

But just because I was willing to address my patients' pain didn't mean I knew how. One thing I was sure of: I was on my own. There were no books I could read, no experts I could correspond with, no training programs I could apply to. All I had to go on was my instincts. I didn't know it yet, but they were about to lead me to a whole new source of information.

My instincts led me into the present. That's where my patients' suffering was. Taking them back to their past was just a distraction; I didn't want any more Tonys. The past has memories, emotions, and insights, all of which have value. But I was looking for something powerful enough to bring relief right now. To find it, I had to stay in the present.

I had only one rule: every time a patient asked for relief—from hurt feelings, self-consciousness, demoralization, or anything else—I had to address it then and there. I had to come up with something on the spot. Working without a net, I got in the habit of saying out loud whatever occurred to me that might help the patient. It was kind of like Freud's free association in reverse—done by the doctor instead of the patient. I'm not sure he would have approved.

I got to the point where I could talk without knowing what I was going to say next. It began to feel as though some other force was speaking through me. Little by little, the tools in this book (and the philosophy behind them) made themselves known. The only standard they had to meet was that they worked.

Since I never considered my search complete until I had a specific tool to offer a patient, it's crucial to understand exactly what I mean when I use the term *tool*. A tool is much more than an "attitude adjustment." If changing your life were only a matter of adjusting your attitude, you wouldn't need this book. Real change requires you to change your behavior—not just your attitude.

Let's say you scream when you get frustrated—you let loose on your spouse, your kids, your employees. Someone helps you realize how unseemly this is, how it's damaging your relationships. You now have a new attitude about screaming. You may feel enlightened and better about yourself . . . until an employee makes a costly mistake. At which point you start screaming without even thinking.

A change in attitude won't stop you from screaming because attitudes can't control behavior; they're not strong enough. To control behavior you need a specific procedure to use at a specific time to combat a specific problem. That's what a tool is.

You'll have to wait (without screaming if you can) until Chapter 3 to learn the tool that applies here. The point is that a tool—unlike an attitude adjustment—requires you to do something. Not only does it take work, it's work you have to do over and over again—every time you get frustrated. A new attitude means nothing unless followed by a change in behavior. The surest way to change behavior is with a tool.

Beyond what I've said so far, there's a more crucial difference between a tool and an attitude. An attitude consists of thoughts happening inside your head—even if you change it, you're working within the limitations you already have. The most profound value of a tool is that it takes you beyond what happens inside your head. It connects you to a world infinitely bigger than you are, a world of limitless forces. It doesn't matter whether you call this the collective unconscious or the spiritual world. I found it simplest to call it the "higher world," and the forces it contains I call "higher forces."

Because I needed the tools to have such power, it took a great deal of effort to develop them. The information would emerge in a crude, unfinished form at first. I'd have to rework a tool hundreds of times. My patients never complained; in fact, they liked being part of creating something. They were always willing to test-drive a new version of a tool and come back and tell me what had worked and what hadn't. All they asked is that the tool help them.

The process made me vulnerable to them. I couldn't hold myself at a distance like an all-knowing authority figure handing down information from on high. This work was more of a joint effort—which was actually a relief. I was never comfortable with the traditional therapy model where the patient was "ill" and the therapist, holding him at arm's length like a dead fish, would "cure" him. This always offended me—I didn't feel I was any better than my patients.

What I enjoyed as a therapist wasn't holding the patient at a distance; it was putting power into my patients' hands. Teaching them the tools was my way of giving them the ultimate gift—the ability to change their lives. That made it tremendously satisfying each time a tool was fully developed.

In the process of developing the tools, it would be surprisingly clear when a tool was fully formed. It never felt like I made it up out of thin air; I had the distinct impression that I was uncovering something that already existed. What I did bring to the table was faith that, for each problem I could identify, there was a tool to be discovered that would bring relief. I was like a dog with a bone until the tool appeared.

That faith was about to be rewarded in a way I never could have imagined.

As time went by, I observed what happened to patients who used the tools regularly. As I'd hoped, they were now able to control their symptoms: panic, negativity, avoidance, etc. But something else—something unexpected—was happening. They began to develop new abilities. They were able to express themselves more confidently; they experienced a level of creativity they'd never felt before; they found themselves emerging as leaders. They were having an impact on the world around them—often for the first time in their lives.

I'd never set out to do this. I had defined my job as returning the patient to "normal." But these patients were going far beyond normal—developing potential they didn't even know they had. The same tools that relieved pain in the present, when used over time, were affecting every part of their lives. The tools were turning out to be even more powerful than I'd hoped.

To make sense out of this, I had to expand my focus beyond the tools themselves and take a closer look at the higher forces they were releasing. I'd seen these forces at work before. So have you—every human being has experienced them. They have a hidden, unexpected power that lets us do things we usually think of as impossible. But, for most people, the only time we have access to them is in an emergency. Then, we can act with heightened courage and resourcefulness—but as soon as the emergency is over, the powers go away; we forget we even have them.

My patients' experiences opened my eyes to a completely new vision of human potential. My patients were functioning as if they had access to these forces every day. Using the tools, the forces could be generated at will. This discovery revolutionized my view of how psychotherapy should work. Instead of seeing problems as an expression of a "condition" whose cause was in the past, we needed to see them as catalysts for developing forces that were already present, lying dormant inside us.

But the therapist had to do more than just see the problems as catalysts. His job was to give the patient concrete access to the forces that were needed to solve the problems. These forces had to be *felt,* not just talked about. That required something therapy had never provided: a set of tools.

I had just spent an hour pouring out a tremendous amount of information. Barry had taken it all in stride, nodding vigorously at points. There was only one fly in the ointment. I noticed that every time I mentioned "forces" he looked doubtful. I knew he wasn't good at hiding what he was thinking—I got ready for the inevitable interrogation.

Most of what Phil had said was revelatory. I absorbed it like a sponge and was ready to use it on my patients. But there was one point I couldn't swallow: it was the part about these higher forces he kept referring to. He was asking me to believe in something that couldn't be measured or even seen. I was pretty sure I'd hidden these doubts from him. Then he interrupted my thoughts.

"Something's bothering you."

"No, nothing . . . that was amazing."

He just stared at me. The last time I felt like this was when I got caught putting sugar on my cereal as a kid. "All right. Just one little thing . . . okay, it isn't so little. Are you absolutely sure about these higher forces?"

He certainly looked sure. Then, he asked me, "Did you ever make a big change in your life—like a quantum leap where you went way past what you thought you could do?"

As a matter of fact, I had. Although I had tried hard to forget it, I'd started my professional life as a lawyer. By age twenty-two, I had gained admission to one of the best law schools in the country. By age twenty-five, I had graduated near the top of my class and was hired immediately by a prestigious law firm. Having conquered the system, I stood at the top of the mountain—and I hated it right away. It was stuffy, conservative, and boring. I constantly fought the urge to quit. But I'd pushed myself really hard all my life; quitting wasn't in my repertoire. How would I explain quitting a powerful, well-compensated profession—especially to my parents, who'd encouraged me to be an attorney my whole life?

But somehow I did quit. I remembered the day very well. I was twenty-eight years old, standing in the lobby of the office building where I worked, staring into the silent, glazed-over faces passing by on the sidewalk outside. For a moment, to my horror, I saw my own face in the reflection of the window. My eyes looked dead. Suddenly I felt I was in jeopardy of losing everything and becoming one of those gray-suited zombies. Then, just as suddenly, I felt something I'd never felt before: a force of absolute conviction, absolute confidence. Without any effort on my part, I felt it carry me right into my boss's office. I quit on the spot. When I looked back on what happened with Phil's question in mind, I realized I *had* been propelled by a force that came from someplace else.

As I described this to Phil, he got excited. He pointed at me and said, "*That's* what I'm talking about. You felt a higher force in action. People have these experiences all the time, but they don't understand what they're feeling." He paused and asked, "You didn't plan for that to happen, right?"

I shook my head.

"Can you imagine what your life would be like if you could tap into that force at will? That's what the tools give you."

I still couldn't fully accept the idea of higher forces, but it didn't matter. Whatever you called the force that allowed me to change my life—I knew it was real. I had felt it. If the tools gave me access to it every day, I didn't care what you called it. And when I introduced the tools to my patients, they didn't care either. Thrilled with the possibility that I could truly help change their lives, I was radiating an enthusiasm you can't fake. That got their attention in a way nothing else ever had.

The feedback was uniformly positive. Many commented on how much more productive the sessions seemed. "Normally, I'd leave here in a fog, not sure I'd gotten anything out of the session. Now, I leave here feeling like there's something I can do—*something practical that will help me.*" For the first time in my short career, I felt able to instill hope in my patients. It changed everything. I began to hear a familiar refrain—"You've given me more in one session than I've gotten in years of therapy." My practice quickly grew. I was feeling more fulfilled than ever before. And sure enough, I noticed the same changes in my patients that Phil saw when he was discovering the tools. Their lives were expanding in unexpected ways. They were becoming better leaders, better parents; they were bolder in every area of their lives.

Twenty-five years have passed since Phil and I met. The tools delivered exactly what he said they would: a daily connection to life-changing higher forces. The more I used the tools, the more clearly I felt that these forces came *through me*, not *from me*—they were a gift from somewhere else. They carried an extraordinary power that made it possible to do things I'd never done before. Over time, I was able to accept that these new powers were given to me by higher forces. Not only have I experienced these forces for two and a half decades, I've had the privilege of training patients to access them just as consistently.

The purpose of this book is to give you the same access. These forces will revolutionize the way you look at your life and your problems. The problems won't scare or overwhelm you anymore. Instead of asking, "Is there anything I can do about that problem?" you'll learn to ask a very different question: "Which tool allows me to solve it?"

Between the two of us, Phil and I have sixty years of psychotherapy experience. Based on this experience, we've identified four fundamental problems that keep people from living the lives they want to live. How much happiness and satisfaction you get out of life will depend on how well you can free yourself from those problems. Each of the next four chapters addresses one of these. Each chapter also provides you with the tool that works most effectively on that problem. We'll explain how the tool connects you to a higher force—and we'll explain how that force solves your problem.

You may not see your problems exactly reflected in the struggles of the patients we discuss. Fortunately, that doesn't mean you can't take advantage of the tools. You'll find that they'll help you in a variety of situations. To make that perfectly clear, at the end of each chapter we'll describe what we call "Other Uses" for each tool. You'll probably find at least one of these that applies to your life. What we've found is that the four higher forces the tools evoke are basic necessities for a fulfilling life. It matters less what form your problem takes than that you use the tools.

We're confident about everything in this book because it's been developed and tested through real experience. But don't take our word for it; read it skeptically. As you do, you might find yourself questioning some of the ideas. We've heard most of these questions before, and toward the end of each chapter we'll answer the most common ones. But the real answers are in the tools; using them will allow you to experience the effect of higher forces. We've found that once people have experienced this repeatedly, their objections disappear.

Since the bottom line is getting you to use the tools, at the end of each chapter you'll find a very short summary of the problem, the tool, and how to use it. If you're serious about using the tools, you'll return to these summaries over and over again to stay on course.

By the time you've finished the next four chapters, you will have learned the four tools that will enable you to live a fulfilling life. You might think this is all you need. It's not. It may surprise you, but most people stop using the tools even though they work. This is one of the most maddening things about human nature: we quit doing the things that help us the most.

We're really serious about helping you change your life. If you feel the same way, you're going to have to overcome your resistance. This is where the rubber meets the road. In order to succeed, you'll need to understand what stops you from using the tools—and you'll need a way to fight back. Chapter 6 tells you how. It gives you a fifth tool, in some ways the most crucial one. This is the tool that makes sure you'll keep using the other four.

There's one more thing you'll need to make absolutely certain you don't give up on using the tools to connect with higher forces. Faith. Higher forces are so mysterious that it's almost impossible *not* to doubt their existence from time to time. Some would even call this the existential issue of the modern age—how to have faith in something completely intangible. In my case, I imbibed doubt and disbelief with my mother's milk because both of my parents were atheists. They would've laughed at the word *faith*, let alone anything like "higher forces" that couldn't be explained rationally or scientifically. Chapter 7 will document my struggle to place my trust in these forces and help you to do the same.

Believe me, if I learned to have faith, anyone can.

I assumed that accepting higher forces as real was the final leap I'd have to take. I was wrong. Phil had one more crazy idea up his sleeve. He claimed that every time anyone used a tool, the higher forces evoked would benefit not just the individual, but everyone around him or her. Over the years, this seemed less and less crazy. I came to believe that higher forces were more than just beneficial to society—we couldn't survive without them. You needn't take my word for this. Chapter 8 gives you a way to experience it for yourself.

The health of our society depends on the efforts of each

individual. Every time one of us gains access to higher forces, all of us benefit. That places a special responsibility on those who know how to use the tools. They become the first to bring higher forces to the rest of the society. They are pioneers, building a new, reinvigorated community.

I wake up every morning grateful that higher forces are there. They never stop revealing themselves in new ways. Through this book we share their magic with you. We're excited about the journey you're about to undertake.

CHAPTER 2

The Tool:
The Reversal of Desire

The Higher Force:
The Force of Forward Motion

VINNY WAS A PATIENT OF MINE WITH A QUESTION-able gift: he could turn almost anyone against him within minutes of their meeting. At our first session, I greeted him in the waiting room, and he barked sarcastically: "Hey, great decor—get this shit at a yard sale? IKEA would be a big step up for you." When he wasn't using his wit to alienate people, he was actually a talented stand-up comic. But you wouldn't know it by his résumé. When I met him, he was thirty-three, he'd been doing stand-up comedy for over ten years, and he'd never broken out of the small-club circuit.

It wasn't for lack of opportunity. His manager had devoted himself to getting Vinny into successful venues—

bigger clubs, talk shows, sitcoms. Despite stiff competition for these opportunities, Vinny had a good shot. He was very funny. The trouble was he kept sabotaging his manager's efforts. In one incident, his manager had set up a meeting with a big-time club owner, the kind that can make or break careers—and Vinny hadn't shown up; he hadn't even called to explain or reschedule. That was the last straw for his manager, who threatened to fire Vinny unless he saw me. "I decided I might as well go through the motions," Vinny said, winking conspiratorially.

I asked Vinny why he no-showed. His excuse—the first of many—was ludicrous. "I'm not a morning person," he complained in an aggrieved tone, "and my manager knows it."

"Couldn't you have made an exception this time when it meant so much for your career?"

Vinny shook his beefy head definitively. "No. I'm not getting on that frantic 'do-anything-for-your-career' treadmill. Too much stress."

If getting up in the morning was too taxing, it was no wonder Vinny's career was stalled. The missed meeting was only the latest instance of self-sabotage. In another fiasco, his manager booked him into a large amphitheater for a charity fund-raising event. His act started strong, but Vinny was booed off the stage when he started telling offensive jokes. He seemed to relish putting people off. When his manager got him invited to a hip Hollywood party where Vinny could've courted the people who made hiring decisions for TV sitcoms, Vinny showed up drunk, disheveled, and smelling of vomit.

"Did you ever ask yourself why you're deliberately blowing up your career?" I asked.

"I'm not blowing up anything. I just won't sell out. You kiss someone's ass at a party, it seems harmless enough. Maybe they do you a favor. Soon you're censoring your best stuff. You end up telling 'penguin-at-a-bar' jokes just to make yourself user-friendly."

If *user-friendly* meant showing up to meetings on time, then it was exactly what he needed to become, but that wasn't how Vinny saw it.

"My job is to be funny, not friendly. If you want 'friendly,' hire a guy who thinks mayo on white bread is a great meal. I'll even donate the brown paper bag so he can bring it to work."

Vinny was giving a clinic in how to destroy a career. Worse, he'd convinced himself he was acting out of a sense of virtue. I called his bluff.

"I guess you've got it figured out. I think you should go back to your manager and tell him you'll be fine without him; you're happy with the level you're at. You can arrange your own club dates." I tossed my notepad and pen onto my desk and got up out of my chair. "If we stop the session right now, I won't even charge you for it."

Vinny's eyes widened. "B-But I . . . ," he stammered, "I

thought we could . . ." He closed his eyes and collected himself. "It's not like I don't *want* to get ahead."

"Then how about being honest about why you keep blowing it?"

It took a while, but he finally admitted that he hated situations where his fortunes depended on other people: interviews, auditions, even a phone call to someone who might be able to help his career. These situations made him vulnerable, and he avoided them like the plague.

I asked him what was so bad about needing something from others.

"I hate it," he growled. After some questioning, he revealed why. "I came out of the womb with a clown suit on, performing loudly, to get attention. As a kid I would constantly try out new material on my father's customers. It drove him crazy."

"Why?"

"He ran his business out of the house."

"What kind of business?"

"He was an undertaker."

I laughed. "C'mon, Vinny. Be serious."

"I *am* being serious. Every day I'd sneak into the waiting room and do my act, and every evening I got strapped with a belt. If I broke down and cried, he'd call me a 'fairy' and strap me harder." His eyes started to tear up. "It was a fucking nightmare."

It became clear why he'd do anything to avoid being in

a vulnerable situation. He never wanted to give anyone else the chance to inflict pain on him again. But he'd paid a steep price for this —he'd sacrificed his career.

You may not have made the same kind of sacrifice Vinny had. But I've never met anyone who hasn't given up *something* in order to avoid pain.

THE COMFORT ZONE

Avoiding pain wouldn't be a problem if we did it once or twice a year. But for most of us, it's a deeply ingrained habit. We barricade ourselves behind an invisible wall and don't venture out because beyond the wall is pain. This safe space is called the "Comfort Zone." In the most extreme cases, people hide behind the actual walls of their home, afraid to venture into the outside world. That's what it means to be agoraphobic. But for most of us, the Comfort Zone isn't a physical place; it's a way of life that avoids anything that might be painful.

Vinny's Comfort Zone consisted of situations where he felt safe: small clubs where he knew he had a steady gig, a small circle of friends from high school who laughed at all his jokes, a girlfriend who would never leave him no matter what he demanded of her. He avoided doing anything that made him feel exposed: auditioning for a bigger job, associating with people who could help his career, dating a woman who had a life of her own.

Your Comfort Zone might not be as obvious as Vinny's, but you have one—we all do. Let's see what yours is like. Try the following exercise (all exercises are best done with your eyes closed):

> Pick something you hate doing. It could be traveling, meeting new people, family gatherings, etc. How do you organize your life so you can avoid doing it? Imagine that pattern is a place you hide in. That's your Comfort Zone. What does it feel like?

You probably felt you were in a safe and familiar place, free of the pain the world brings with it. This almost completely re-creates your Comfort Zone, but it leaves out the final ingredient. Strange as it might seem, merely escaping pain isn't enough for us. We insist that the pain be replaced with pleasure.

We do this with an endless array of addictive activities: Internet surfing, drugs and alcohol, pornography, the aptly named "comfort food." Even manic gambling and shopping are pleasures of a sort. All these behaviors are widespread—we're an entire culture looking for its Comfort Zone

We weave these activities into our daily routines. Vinny, for example, spent every evening getting high with the same friends, eating pizza, and playing video games. He described this time as if he'd entered an alternate universe. "One hit and the rest of the world disappears."

This alternate world feels like a soothing, pleasurable warm bath, as if, for a moment, you've found your way back to the womb. These "warm-bath" activities just cripple us further. The more you hide in the warm bath, the less willing you become to deal with the cold shower of reality.

Ask yourself what your own warm-bath activities are. The more frequently you indulge in them, the more likely it is that you're using them to create a Comfort Zone. Now try the following exercise:

> Feel yourself indulging in one or more of these behaviors. Imagine the pleasure you feel lifts you into a womb-like world. How does this world affect your sense of purpose?

Whatever your Comfort Zone consists of, you pay a huge price for it. Life provides endless possibilities, but along with them comes pain. If you can't tolerate pain, you can't be fully alive. There are many different examples of this. If you're shy and avoid people, then you lose the vitality that comes with a sense of community. If you're creative but can't tolerate criticism, then you avoid selling your ideas to the marketplace. If you're a leader but you can't confront people, no one will follow you.

The Comfort Zone is supposed to keep your life safe, but what it really does is keep your life small. Vinny was a good example. Every area of life—his career, friendships, even his romantic life—was a shrunken miniature of what it could have been.

Here's a way to picture the Comfort Zone and the price you pay for living in it:

Most of us are like the stick figure, stuck inside the Comfort Zone. To take advantage of the endless possibilities that life provides us, we have to venture out. The first thing we meet is pain. Without a way to get through it, we scurry back to safety. This is depicted in the arrow that goes out, comes close to pain, and turns back again. Eventually, we give up on ever escaping the Comfort Zone; our most treasured dreams and aspirations are lost. Nineteenth-century physician, teacher, and author Oliver Wendell Holmes in "The Voiceless" wrote: "Alas for those that never sing, / But die with all their music in them."

It is a tragedy to die with your song unsung. What's worse is that *we* are guilty of stilling our own voices—*we silence ourselves.* Yet despite the terrible price we pay, we don't leave the Comfort Zone. Why not?

Because we're held there by the classic modern weakness: the need for immediate gratification. The Comfort Zone makes us feel good in the moment. Who cares what the future penalty will be? But the penalty does come, bringing with it the worst pain of all—the knowledge that you've wasted your life.

We're trained as a society to expect, even demand, immediate gratification. And we have an extraordinary ability to rationalize this weakness. Instead of admitting we're avoiding pain, we tell ourselves we're being virtuous; Vinny had convinced himself he was refusing to "sell out." We end up with a distorted worldview that makes avoidance seem right, even brave and idealistic. This is the worst sin of all—lying to ourselves. It makes change impossible.

I explained all of this to Vinny. Just having an understanding of why he was so stuck made him feel a little better. He thanked me and started bustling out the door.

"Not so fast," I said. Vinny looked startled. "I'm glad you feel better," I said, "but if we leave it at that, nothing will have changed; you'll still be stuck in the Comfort Zone. Do you want to accept that penalty?"

"If you'll let me leave now—yeah," Vinny answered,

half-joking. But he sat back down again. For the first time, I saw in his eyes the hope that his life could be better than it was.

THE HIGHER FORCE: FORWARD MOTION

A few rare individuals refuse to live limited lives. They drive through tremendous amounts of pain—from rejections and failures to shorter moments of embarrassment and anxiety. They also handle the small, tedious pain required for personal discipline, forcing themselves to do things we all know we should do but don't—like exercising, eating right, and staying organized. Because they avoid nothing, they can pursue their highest aspirations. They seem more alive than the rest of us.

They have something that gives them the strength to endure pain—a sense of purpose. What they do in the present, no matter how painful, has meaning in terms of what they want for the future. The avoider only cares about immediate gratification; he takes no responsibility for his future.

A sense of purpose doesn't come from thinking about it. It comes from taking action that moves you toward the future. The moment you do this, you activate a force more powerful than the desire to avoid pain. We call this the "Force of Forward Motion."

It's the first of the five higher forces we'll talk about in this book. They're "higher" forces because they exist on the plane where the universe orders and creates, giving them mysterious powers. These powers are invisible, but their effects are all around you. This is most obvious for the Force of Forward Motion.

Its power is the power of life itself. Everything that's alive is evolving into the future with a sense of purpose—from a single organism to a species to the entire planet. Dylan Thomas called it "The force that through the green fuse drives the flower." The continuous existence of life over millions of years is a testament to the invincible strength of the Force of Forward Motion.

Its power has touched your own life as well. You started life as a helpless infant; yet in a remarkably short time, you moved from crawling to standing to walking. You did this despite countless painful setbacks. Watch a child learning to walk now. No matter how many times he falls, he soon picks himself back up to pursue his goal. His sense of purpose is amazing; he's tapped into the Force of Forward Motion.

This force drives children to develop the basic skills they need to grow up. Because it has this identical function in each child, it works as a universal presence they're not aware of. Things are different in adults. The central task of an adult is to find her purpose in the world. This purpose is different for each person—finding it is an individual matter. The Force of Forward Motion only works in an individual if she consciously chooses to use it—and accepts the pain that comes with it.

Most of us choose avoidance instead. As a result, we don't live up to our potential, never becoming fully ourselves. Vinny was a great example. As a child he was driven to develop as a performer; despite the whippings, he performed for his father's customers every day. But as an adult, he decided he didn't want to be vulnerable anymore. That decision made him into a bitter, limited version of who he was meant to be.

Carried away with my own excitement, I told Vinny, "In forward motion, your life becomes like a radiant star, expanding outward. When you're hiding in the Comfort Zone, life becomes a black hole, collapsing into itself."

Vinny didn't share my enthusiasm. "You sound like my Sunday school teacher—who, I happen to know, was an old maid who never got laid. You have no clue what it's like to put your balls on the line in front of a bunch of assholes."

As harsh as this sounded, I understood it. For Vinny, the Force of Forward Motion was just a bunch of words. He needed to *feel* that force move him from the inside before he could have any faith in it.

As far as I was concerned this visceral experience was precisely what was missing from traditional psychotherapy. Therapy could elicit ideas and emotions—but it had no direct way to connect patients to the forces they needed to change their lives. When I met Phil, I instantly realized he'd learned how to make that connection. The answer lay in the power of the tools he'd discovered.

The tools were designed to take advantage of the unusual nature of higher forces. We're used to forces we can control: we step on the gas, switch on the light, turn on the hot water, and get the response we want. These forces are separate from us, we control them from the outside. It doesn't matter what state we're in ourselves.

That won't work with higher forces; they're not subject to outside control. To harness a higher force, you have to become one with it. You do that by taking on the same form the force takes—making yourself into a miniversion of it. No amount of thinking can do this for you; you need to change your state of being.

That's the genius of the tools. Each tool in this book lets you "imitate" the workings of a different higher force, putting you at one with it and tapping its energy. The book explains the nature of the five basic higher forces. Then, for each force, it teaches you the tool that aligns you with it. With practice, you'll be able to summon these forces at will. They'll give you something priceless—the ability to create your own future.

THE TOOL: THE REVERSAL OF DESIRE

We've chosen to make the Force of Forward Motion the first higher force we discussed because its nature is the most obvious, moving relentlessly through the universe with a sense of purpose. To tap into this force, *you* need to move relentlessly forward in your own life—only then have you taken on its form.

But doing that is not so easy. By now, you know we avoid the pain of forward motion at all costs. Phil seemed undaunted by this nasty human weakness. He told me—with complete confidence—that anyone could master their fear of pain. I asked him what made him so certain. He replied that he'd discovered a tool that trained you to *desire pain*.

This sounded strange, even for Phil. I wondered if he was some kind of a masochist—or worse. Then he told me the following story and I saw the method to his madness.

I was a sophomore in high school at age thirteen—a skinny runt in an all-male student body, every one of whom seemed to tower over me. The most dreaded part of the week was the mechanical drawing class. My drawings were big smudges—they looked like Rorschach tests.

More terrifying than the class was the student sitting next to me. Thick and hairy, he was the eighteen-year-old captain and star running back of the football team. I looked at him as if he were a mixture of a god and a very dangerous animal. Fortunately, we had at least one thing in common—we were the two worst draftsmen in the class. As we bonded over our incompetence, he opened up to me.

He talked about the subject closest to his heart—football. He was first team All-City, considered the best running back in the area. For whatever reason, he was eager to explain to me how he'd achieved this distinction.

What he said shocked me—I can still remember it forty years later. He explained that he wasn't the fastest back in the city, nor was he the most elusive. There were stronger players, too. But he was still the best in the city, with big-time scholarship offers to prove it. The reason he was the best, he explained, had nothing to do with his physical abilities—it was his attitude about getting hit.

He'd demand the ball on the first play from scrimmage and would run at the nearest tackler. He wouldn't try to fake him out or run out of bounds. He'd run right at him and get hit on purpose, no matter how much it hurt. "When I get up, I feel great, alive. That's why I'm the best. The other runners are afraid, you can see it in their eyes." He was right; none of them shared his desire to get crushed by a defender.

My first reaction was that he was mad. He lived in a world of constant pain and danger—and he liked it. It was exactly the world I'd spent my young life avoiding.

But I couldn't get his crazy idea out of my mind; if you go right for the pain, you develop superpowers. The more the years went by, the more I found this to be true—and not just in sports.

Without knowing it, he'd introduced me to the secret of mastering pain—and given me the basis for the tool that could connect anyone to the Force of Forward Motion.

That football player stood out from his peers because he "reversed" the normal human desire to avoid pain—he wanted pain. This came naturally to him but seems impossible to the average person. It's not. With the right tool, anyone can train themselves to desire pain.

The tool is called the "Reversal of Desire." Before you try it, pick a situation you're avoiding. It needn't involve physical pain the way it did for the football player. More likely, you're avoiding some kind of emotional pain; a phone call you're putting off, a project that seems overwhelming, or a task that's simply tedious. Vinny was avoiding the rejection he'd have to face if he reached higher in show business.

Once you've chosen a situation, imagine the pain you'd feel. Then, forget the situation and focus on the pain itself. Then try using the tool.

The Reversal of Desire

See the pain appear in front of you as a cloud. Scream silently at the cloud, "BRING IT ON!" Feel an intense desire for the pain to move you into the cloud.

Scream silently, "I LOVE PAIN!" as you keep moving forward. Go so deeply into the pain you're at one with it.

You will feel the cloud spit you out and close behind you. Say inwardly with conviction, "PAIN SETS ME FREE!" As you leave the cloud, feel yourself propelled forward into a realm of pure light.

The first two steps require activating your own will, but in the final step, you should feel carried by a force much bigger than you are: that's the Force of Forward Motion.

When you "bring on" the pain, make it as extreme as you can. What would it feel like if you got the very worst outcome? The audience boos your speech. Your spouse walks out on you in the middle of the confrontation. If you can master the worst, then anything less becomes easy. The more intense the pain—and the more aggressively you move into it—the more energy you'll create.

Learn to go through the three steps quickly but intensely. Don't just do it once. Repeat the steps over and over until you feel you've thoroughly converted all the pain to energy. You can remember each step by the phrase that goes with it.

1. "Bring it on."
2. "I love pain."
3. "Pain sets me free."

Just saying the three phrases will help you.

Now it should be clear why we call the tool the Reversal of Desire. You've taken your normal desire to avoid pain and reversed it into a desire to face it.

HOW THE REVERSAL OF DESIRE MASTERS PAIN

Using the tool regularly reveals the secret about pain that allows you to master it: pain is not absolute. *Your experience of pain changes relative to how you react to it.* When you move toward it, pain shrinks. When you move away from it, pain grows. If you flee from it, pain pursues you like a monster in a dream. If you confront the monster, it goes away.

That's why desire is a crucial part of the tool. It keeps you moving toward pain. You're not desiring pain because you're masochistic; you're desiring pain so you can shrink it. When you become confident you can do this every time, you've mastered your fear of pain.

The diagram below illustrates how this process works. This time, when the figure leaves the Comfort Zone, he has a completely different mind-set. Not only isn't he trying to avoid pain, *he desires it*. It's this desire that puts him in motion; as I've said, when you're moving toward it, pain shrinks and becomes less intimidating. You can now move through it into an expanded world of endless possibility.

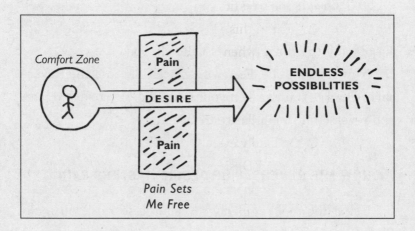

My father gave me my first lesson in the power of moving into pain when he taught me to bodysurf. He started by showing me how to get into frigid water. You have to dive in all at once, without thinking. He and I would sprint down the beach as fast as we could and then dive as deep as we could. It was a shock, but we'd be bodysurfing while the other swimmers were still torturing themselves trying to inch their way into the water. Looking back, I realize that's the first time I was ever encouraged to move toward pain voluntarily.

WHEN TO USE THE REVERSAL OF DESIRE

I walked Vinny through the Reversal of Desire in my office many times until I was confident he'd be able to use the tool on his own. "It makes me feel kind of pumped up, like I've been working out," he admitted. "So when am I supposed to do this?"

That was a good question, and one that applies to each of the tools we present in this book. Just as important as learning a tool is knowing when to use it. We've found that this can't be left to chance. For every tool, there is a set of easily recognizable moments that call for its use. We call these "cues," just like a cue that triggers an actor to say his lines. Use the tool immediately every time you recognize a cue.

For the Reversal of Desire, the first cue is obvious—right before you're about to do something you want to avoid. Let's say you have to call someone who intimidates you, or you really need to get down to work, but you feel restless and distracted. At these moments, focus on the exact pain you'd feel if you began the action. Use the tool on that pain (multiple times if necessary) until you can feel the energy of the final step carrying you forward. Don't stop to think—let it lead you right into taking the action you were avoiding.

The second cue isn't as obvious because it occurs in your thoughts. We all share the same bad habit. When we have to do something we find extremely unpleasant, we start thinking about it rather than doing it: Why do I have to do it? I can't do it, I'll do it next week, etc. Thinking can't help you act in the face of pain; in fact, it usually makes you even more avoidant. The only way your thoughts can help you master pain is if they trigger you to use the Reversal of Desire. This is the second cue: each time you catch yourself thinking about the dreaded task, stop thinking and use the tool.

This cue trains you to use the tool *right now*. No matter how far away the action is, the force you need to move forward can be generated only in the present. Each time you use this second cue, you're making a deposit in an invisible bank account; but you're depositing energy, not money— eventually you'll build up enough to act.

Vinny had the opportunity to test this out. Part of cleaning up his life required a call to the powerful club owner he'd blown off. It was intimidating enough asking him for a job, but now he also had to ask for his forgiveness. Vinny's cue to use the Reversal of Desire was every time he thought, *No way, I can't do it.* After two weeks of doing this, he shocked himself and made the call. The guy didn't get back to him for five days, which gave Vinny a chance to use the cue hundreds of times more.

Finally, the dreaded return call came. The owner chewed Vinny out. "It was the longest five fucking minutes of my life," Vinny said. Then the owner got another incoming call and put Vinny on hold "for another five fucking minutes." Vinny used the Reversal of Desire for dear life, expecting more abuse—but the other call was a cancellation by a comic for that very night. The club owner offered the slot to Vinny—who "killed." The turn of events stunned Vinny—or, as he put it, "Dumb luck, huh?"

THE SECRET BENEFIT: TURNING PAIN INTO POWER

In truth, it wasn't luck at all. I've seen it over and over again; a patient puts some real effort into moving forward and all of a sudden, people and opportunities appear as if by magic to help him along the way.

I experienced this in my own life before I ever learned about the tools. For me, the automatic prestige and high pay of a legal career was a gilded cage—its own kind of Comfort Zone. To get my life moving forward again, I had to leave my law firm. I decided to become a psychotherapist, but I knew it would require four years to get fully credentialed. How was I going to support myself during this time? Not expecting much, I sent my résumé out to dozens of attorneys, asking for part-time work. Most of them turned me down. Just when I was beginning to get desperate, I got a call out of the blue from an attorney who'd attended the same law school as I did. He was a godsend. He let me work as many or as few hours as I wanted. He even introduced me to divorce law, a field in which I could already begin to hone my psychotherapeutic skills. I couldn't have made the transition without his help.

From the beginning of my psychotherapy practice, I was sure something was missing from my training. I wasn't helping people as much as I knew I could. I kept looking for someone to show me the ropes. Despite repeated disappointments, I was determined to keep looking. That was what led me to attend the seminar Phil taught. Clearly, for me, meeting him represented one of those "lucky" events. He never hesitated to answer my questions—and I peppered him with thousands of them; and unlike others, he never took it personally or shied away from me if I challenged the answers he gave me. Talking to him was like having an interactive encyclopedia with answers to questions I'd asked my entire life.

If these chance meetings and sudden opportunities aren't luck, what are they? The twentieth-century Scottish explorer W. H. Murray described it this way: "The moment one definitely commits oneself, then Providence moves too . . . raising in one's favor all manner of unforeseen incidents and meetings and material assistance, which no man could have dreamt would have come his way."

Providence is an antiquated term, but it's the right one. It connotes the support and guidance that come from something greater than yourself. What Murray was saying was that your forward motion puts you in sync with the greater movement of the universe—enabling you to avail yourself of the myriad opportunities it can provide you. This unforeseen assistance is one of the many benefits that higher forces can grant you. It's subject to the same rules we discussed earlier: you can't control these forces from the outside; you have to become like them in order to tap into their energy.

It's easy to oversimplify this. A patient of mine toiled over many long nights and weekends to formulate a unique and creative proposal for his boss, but when he finally worked up the courage to submit the idea, his boss rejected it. "You told me that if I moved forward, the universe would help me," he complained.

This response illustrates how the modern mind typically misunderstands spiritual forces. It wants to make them predictably controllable. Yes, moving forward is a powerful way to connect to higher forces. But those forces are ultimately a mystery; they work in ways that are often beyond immediate understanding. The universe won't reward you like a trained seal every time you move forward. In fact, the naive belief that it would is simply another version of the Comfort Zone.

As patients learn to work with higher forces, they encounter yet another mystery. They feel their powers growing when seemingly out of nowhere something bad happens. Often they're indignant, as if their connection to higher forces was supposed to magically immunize them from adversity.

This reaction is a kind of spiritual immaturity. A true adult accepts that there's a fundamental difference between the goals we have for ourselves and the goals the universe has for us. In general, human beings want to succeed in the outer world—build a successful business, say, or find a life partner. In contrast, the universe doesn't care about our external success; its goal is to develop our *inner strength*. We care about what we achieve on the outside; *the universe is interested in who we are on the inside.*

This explains why adversity doesn't stop even after we move forward; adversity is the only way the universe can increase our inner strength. Everyone understands that, to develop a muscle, you must subject the muscle to resistance—in the form of a heavy weight. Essentially, adversity is the "weight" against which you develop your *inner strength.*

I've witnessed the incredible fortitude people can acquire when they struggle with adversity. I treated a woman whose husband handled all their financial affairs; after he died, she faced the daunting task of mastering the rudiments of finance. Yet within a year of his death, she not only started a successful business, she also became less passive in all her relationships. I've even seen it in kids: an adolescent girl takes refuge in her one friendship with the social-climbing queen bee who dumps her in an abrupt text message—"I'm tired of pretending to be your friend." Her mother worries that this will be a traumatic event from which she'll never recover. Instead, the girl is forced to reach out to other girls and finds that she's quite popular on her own. Her friendships deepen and her self-esteem actually grows.

There's a hidden, inner strength that you cannot find unless you push yourself through adversity. Friedrich

Nietzsche, a daring thinker of the late nineteenth century, put it best in his famous aphorism: "Whatever does not kill me makes me stronger." His idea that adversity has a positive value was new.

When I quoted Nietzsche to Vinny, however, he rolled his eyes and shot back, "Listen, Harvard, I'm not as stupid as I look. I know a little bit about Nietzsche; he *talked* a good game, but he didn't exactly live like Indiana Jones." Vinny had a point—Nietzsche was practically a hermit.

That should come as no surprise. Philosophy is created by intellectuals who rarely ask themselves how to apply their ideas in real life. When your basement floods, or your spouse walks out on you, your thoughts don't turn to Nietzsche. We all have the same reaction at those moments: "This shouldn't be happening to me."

As natural as this reaction seems, it's actually insane: *you're refusing to accept an event that's already happened.* Nothing is a bigger waste of time. The more you complain, the more stuck you become. There's a common term for someone who lets himself wallow in pain like this: a victim.

The victim thinks he knows how the universe should work. When it doesn't treat him the way he "deserves," he concludes the world is against him. This becomes his rationale for giving up and retreating to his Comfort Zone where he can stop trying.

You don't need philosophy to tell you he's not growing or getting stronger.

Nietzsche's statement makes it sound like adversity it-self makes you stronger. It doesn't. Inner strength comes only to those who *move forward* in the face of adversity.

That's impossible for a victim. His energy is wasted in-sisting it shouldn't have happened in the first place. He can't get that energy back until he accepts the event—no matter how painful it was. But *accepting bad things takes work.*

This is where the Reversal of Desire comes in. It by-passes your opinion about *what should be* and gives you an active way to accept *what is.* This differs a bit from using it to prepare you for future pain. You use the tool the same way, but the target pain is in the past (even if it's just a few minutes in the past). In effect, you're training yourself to *desire what's already happened anyway.*

The sooner and more frequently you use the tool when something bad happens, the faster you'll be able to recover. For some people it will be the first time in their lives they've faced adversity without feeling like a victim. With the Re-versal of Desire, Nietzsche's idea becomes a reality.

At least it does with minor adversity—traffic delays or the copy machine breaking down. You begin to recover from these things faster than you thought possible; your frustration tolerance grows. But what about when some-thing really horrible happens? You lose your life savings, a child dies. Is it possible—is it even sane—to accept an event that destroys the fabric of your life?

At least one person has had the authority to answer that question—a famous Austrian psychiatrist named Viktor

Frankl. His authority didn't come from his credentials, however—it came from experiencing the unthinkable. He was enslaved in four Nazi death camps where his mother, father, brother, and wife were killed. Refusing to give up, he became a camp doctor. In that capacity, he fought to sustain the resilience of prisoners who, like him, had lost everything, including their reason to live. He summarized his response to suffering in his book *Man's Search for Meaning*.

His amazing conclusion was that even under indescribably harsh conditions—sleeplessness, starvation, and the ever-present threat of death—there was an opportunity to grow in inner strength. In fact, this was the one thing the Nazis *couldn't* take away from a prisoner. In the camps, the Nazis controlled everything—your possessions, the lives of your loved ones, and ultimately your own life. But the Nazis couldn't strip you of your determination to grow inwardly in whatever time you had left.

As bleak and tenuous as life in the death camps was, Frankl asserted, it still presented "an opportunity and a challenge. One could make a victory of these experiences, turning life into an inner triumph, or one could ignore the challenge and simply vegetate." It was "just such an exceptionally difficult external situation which gives man the opportunity to grow spiritually beyond himself." This inner, spiritual strength at times enabled less hardy prisoners to survive the camps better than those who were physically more robust.

Frankl affirmed what we observed earlier—that whatever your goals are in the outside world, life has its own goals for you. If there is a conflict between these agendas, life will win. In his words, "It did not really matter what we expected from life, but rather what life expected from us." You had to find out what life was asking of you, even if it was simply to bear your suffering with dignity, sacrifice yourself for another, or not to give in to hopelessness for one more day—and then rise to that challenge.

This path develops what's most lacking in our outwardly oriented society: an "inner greatness." We've been conditioned to associate greatness with people who've achieved power or fame in the outside world, such as a Napoleon or a Thomas Edison. We place little value on an *inner greatness* that can be developed by anyone, regardless of his station in life. But it's only this inner greatness that gives meaning to our lives; without it, our society becomes a meaningless shell.

The worship of outer success breeds a selfish fixation on achieving your own goals. Inner greatness, on the other hand, develops only when life makes your goals impossible. You are then faced with a personal, private struggle to reconcile your plans with what life has planned for you. You are forced to become selfless in the best sense—to devote your life to something higher than yourself. Frankl's book is an account of his triumph under the most extreme of such circumstances. His true greatness was in finding meaning in the bleak deprivation of a slave camp—not in his later success as a famous psychiatrist.

FEAR AND COURAGE

The final thing the Reversal of Desire can do for you may be the most important of all—it allows you to develop courage. It always confused me that psychotherapy never addressed the need for courage directly—every patient I've ever had wanted more of it. But like the rest of us, therapists saw it as a kind of mythic power existing only in heroes who were beyond human fear—not a relevant topic for human psychology.

Heroes like that exist only in the movies. Real courage occurs in normal human beings—people with the same fears we all have. Most often, their displays of courage are a mystery—the person himself having no idea how he did it.

Phil saw courage neither as a mythic power nor as a mystery. He defined it in a practical, human way that made it available to anyone. *Courage is the ability to act in the face of fear.* That this seems impossible to most people is because of the way we experience fear.

Fear is almost always linked to an image you have of something terrible happening in the future. If I speak up, I'll get fired. If I start my own business, I'll go bankrupt. The more you fixate on this future image, the more paralyzed you become—unable to act until you are certain the event won't happen. But that kind of certainty is impossible.

It's hard to admit this; our whole culture is based on the lie that it's possible to be certain about the future. Go to the right school, eat the right foods, buy the right stocks, and your future is guaranteed. To develop courage, you have to give up this illusion of future certainty.

This frees you to focus on the present—the only place you can find the courage to act. I'd read about "staying in the present" before I met Phil, but had always considered it a New Age cliché. I reconsidered when he taught me a concrete, step-by-step process for harnessing the power of the present.

The first step is to learn to experience fear without the mental image of the dreaded future event. Focus all your awareness on how the fear feels right now, in the present. When you've separated fear from what you're afraid of in the future, it becomes just another kind of pain you process with the Reversal of Desire.

The tool works the exact same way you've already been using it. You can substitute the word *fear* for *pain* or just remember that fear is a kind of pain. Either way, the energy the Reversal of Desire generates will allow you to take action. With practice, you'll realize it no longer matters what you're afraid of; every instance of fear can be dealt with the same way.

If it seems crazy to desire fear, remember you're not desiring the terrible event, just the feeling of fear it brings up. It's a paradox; only when you desire fear, will you be able to take action in its presence—which is what courage consists of.

But you can't hoard courage. Fear returns quickly, along with the image of the dreaded future event, taking you out of the present. If you're serious about living courageously, condition yourself to use the Reversal of Desire the moment you feel fear. You'll be amazed to find that when this becomes a reflex—and you don't think of the future at all—you'll act with more boldness than you've ever had in your life.

Phil described this as the process of fighting your way back to the present. Staying in the present isn't a state of mystical passivity, it's an *active* process that takes effort. The goal is to be comfortable enough with fear so that you can act. If you want superhuman fearlessness, you can always go to the movies.

FREQUENTLY ASKED QUESTIONS

1. I'm supposed to use the Reversal of Desire every time I do something I'd rather avoid, every time I think about something I'd rather avoid, and every time something bad happens. How do you expect me to do all this work on top of everything else I have going on in my life?

All of the tools we present in this book demand a lot of effort. At some point you'll probably find yourself feeling it's too much. Sometimes we feel too overwhelmed to use the tools, too.

Keep in mind that our whole culture is about getting as much as you can with the least amount of effort. We're going to devote an entire chapter to this subject—Chapter 6. For now, it'll help to understand a weird paradox about the tools: although they require energy at the outset, they *increase* your energy in the long run. So if it seems as though we're asking you to do more than you're already doing, it's because we've seen the results: *life gets easier when you use tools.*

If you're honest, you'll see that without the Reversal of Desire you're stuck in the Comfort Zone with its diminished energy. No matter how difficult you find it is to use the tool, you'll be rewarded ten times over as you leave this paralyzed state. Use it and see for yourself how much better you feel.

Moreover, it takes about three seconds to use a tool. If you use a tool twenty times a day, that's only one minute you've added to your day. Given the incredible results you'll get, we predict you'll find it's a bargain.

2. I followed the instructions for the Reversal of Desire, but I didn't feel anything.

Learning to use the tools is like any other skill. It takes time to master. You wouldn't pick up a violin for the first time and expect to know how to play it.

In our society, we demand immediate results. The moment we don't get them, we tend to quit. Those moments—

when you want to give up—are the moments when it's most important *not* to quit. In fact, you should train yourself to use the Reversal of Desire at the very moment you doubt it the most—not to prove that the tool works, but to develop the right attitude: "When I don't get immediate results, I become even more committed to using the tool." This resolve will give you a period of time in which you can become a true practitioner of the tool. If that level of commitment fails to empower you, then you can stop using the tool knowing you've given it a fair trial.

3. Isn't the tool inviting bad things to happen to me?

This is the most common objection to the Reversal of Desire, but it's also the easiest to refute. Think about it. Who's inviting bad things to happen—the person who's using the Reversal of Desire to confront pain or the person who can't show up for a meeting that's going to change his life?

Nonetheless, people are afraid that by desiring a negative situation, the tool might actually *cause* that situation to occur. We call this the "Southern California objection" because it's rooted in the pop mysticism of the area where we both live and work.

This objection is based on a misunderstanding. The tool trains you to desire the *pain* you associate with a particular event—not the event itself. That's why the instructions direct you to "forget the situation and focus on the pain." The purpose of doing this is to free yourself. If there is a key to influencing the future, it's through bold action.

It may be comforting to believe that your thoughts can directly control future events, but what we've observed is that the patients who believe this most fervently usually want to avoid having to take action.

4. I've gone through enough pain in my life. When is it going to stop?

It's human nature to think you know when you've had enough pain, to want a reprieve from your troubles. But life doesn't work that way. There may be many positive things in your future—great joy and fulfillment. But inevitably, *life will never exempt you from facing more pain.* Once you accept this, your goal will no longer be for pain to stop; it will be to increase your tolerance for it—which is exactly what the Reversal of Desire will do for you.

That leads to a much more positive way to look at pain. Pain is the universe's way of demanding that you continue to learn. The more pain you can tolerate, the more you can learn. In this chapter, what you're learning is how to MOVE FORWARD despite adversity. Every painful event is part of that training program. It's only by accepting this that you can develop your potential to its fullest. Once you look at life this way, you won't ask for pain to stop—because it's really asking for your education to stop.

5. Isn't it masochistic to *desire* pain?

It depends on the kind of pain. There are two different kinds—one necessary and one unnecessary. Necessary pain is the kind you must go through to achieve your goals. If you're a salesman, rejection is necessary pain. Unnecessary pain isn't part of your journey forward. In fact, its purpose is to keep you stuck. That kind of pain is normally called masochistic. The masochist inflicts pain on himself under his own control, and he does it the same way over and over again. He uses the predictable familiarity of his pain of choice to actually keep himself in his Comfort Zone.

6. Why should I use the tool? I don't feel any pain or fear in my life.

We've had patients who say this with a straight face. Sometimes they're lying—they think it's weak to admit that they're hurting or afraid. It usually takes a while to convince them that it's stronger to admit and conquer these feelings than to deny them.

But another group isn't lying; they truly don't feel pain or fear. Unfortunately, that's because they're so deep in the Comfort Zone that they've lost touch with the whole world of possibilities that exist outside the Comfort Zone. This type of person is actually *more* afraid than the average person; they just deal with the fear by *denying there's anything more they want out of life*.

With these people we try to get them to identify new goals. It can be like pulling teeth, but everyone can identify something they don't have that they might want. When we ask them to visualize the specific steps they'd have to go through to reach the goal, there's always at least one step that intimidates them—at that point they're forced to admit they're avoiding pain. They don't know it at the time, but this admission is the first step in coming back to the land of the living.

7. I know somebody who's always moving forward, but I wouldn't want to be like that because they never relax and smell the roses.

That kind of hyperactivity isn't what we mean by forward motion; in fact, it's usually just another form of avoidance. These people are actually using hyperactivity to distract themselves from inner feelings—of terror, failure, or vulnerability. As a result, they can never relax; it's as if they constantly hear footsteps behind them and can't stop running.

Forward motion means something different depending on who you are. The Reversal of Desire gives you the strength to face whatever you're avoiding. Sometimes it's an outer situation, but it's just as possible that it's an inner emotion that makes you uncomfortable.

We've found that people who are non-avoiders actually get *better rest and relaxation* than others. It's only when you face what you're afraid of—inside you or outside you—that your mind can relax. They're less intimidated by the world, more satisfied with their own efforts. This makes them less worried and anxious, so that when it's time to let their hair down, they can turn their minds off; they're not plagued by all the things they're avoiding.

OTHER USES OF THE REVERSAL OF DESIRE

The Reversal of Desire enables you to expand your professional and social circle. *We all know people we'd like to have a connection with but feel insecure about approaching. If you're honest with yourself, you question whether you're really on their level. It's easier to associate only with people who are no threat. This is really a form of avoidance that keeps you from living as fully as you can.*

Marilyn was in her thirties, attractive and alone. She always had a group of guys pursuing her but none of them ever satisfied her. But her real problem was in how she saw the world of men. In her mind, Marilyn split men into an "A" group and a "B" group. She never got to date the A group who in her eyes were more successful and attractive, because when she was introduced to one of them she'd act standoffish. Deep down she was intimidated by them and didn't want them to ask her out. The only men she actually dated were in the B group. Although she complained about their faults, they represented her Comfort Zone. As long as she dated them, there was no chance of her finding someone she was really interested in. Every time she was around the A group she had to use the Reversal of Desire to deal with her anxiety. Eventually she was able to open up to them and act naturally.

The Reversal of Desire enables you to wield authority. *One of the hardest things about being a leader—whether you're the head of a department, an entire business, or even a family—is that you have to make decisions that make people unhappy. That's why they say "it's lonely at the top." An effective leader can tolerate the displeasure of others.*

Elizabeth was a college professor who had just been appointed chairwoman of her department. Although she was nationally known in her field, she was an accessible, modest person. Her nature was to treat everyone as a friend. Everyone liked her—students, professors, even the cleaning staff. But this couldn't continue once she was chairwoman. She could no longer be everyone's friend. She had to sign off on teaching assignments, schedules, vacations, disciplinary issues, etc., and each decision displeased someone. This was so uncomfortable for her that she began to put off decisions until the department fell into chaos. In order to keep her job, she knew she had to force herself to make unpopular decisions. She began to use the Reversal of Desire to deal with the pain of not being liked. She was able to stop being everyone's friend and became an effective leader.

She came to realize that there were leadership issues in every relationship and that often those around her needed her to be a leader as much they needed her to be their friend. As a consequence, all of her relationships improved. Friends and colleagues she'd known for years liked the new clarity and focus she brought to her decisions. Their response gave her a confidence she'd never felt before. Even her parenting improved; now that she was able to set limits for her teenage daughter, their exchanges became more honest, which was a relief to both of them.

The Reversal of Desire overcomes phobias. *A phobia is an irrational fear or dislike of something—like spiders or tight spaces. Its effect is to put certain parts of life out of your reach. Even in mild forms, it can interfere with your functioning at work and in relationships. The tool gives you the courage to put yourself in situations that your anxiety had placed off limits. Life can open up again.*

Michael was an engineer who had to travel all over the country for work. Unfortunately, he'd developed a fear of flying that threatened to end his career. The moment the flight attendant shut the door to the passenger compartment, his breathing would become rapid and his chest would tighten up. Often this would progress to a full-blown panic attack that left him certain he was doomed. At home, just the thought of flying filled him with anticipatory anxiety. He used every excuse he could think of to avoid trips until his problem became obvious to his boss. By using the Reversal of Desire consistently when he became afraid, over time he was able to overcome his flying phobia. Fear was no longer able to stop him.

The Reversal of Desire allows you to develop skills that require a disciplined, long-term commitment. *The biggest difference between those who succeed and those who fail at any endeavor is their level of commitment. Most people would like to be committed. But in practice, commitment requires an endless series of small painful actions. When a person has no way to deal with that pain, his commitment falls apart.*

Jeffrey was a cop who walked a beat. It wasn't what he wanted for a career. Before he'd dropped out of college, he'd been an English major and a good writer. But he knew he'd never reached his writing potential. "My ideas are good. I'm just not sure I can translate them into writing." This had nothing to do with his ability. He'd taken an easy way out—telling stories to fellow cops in bars after work, which was especially easy for him because of the alcohol in his system. But putting the stories down in written form required a much higher degree of commitment. There was pain every step of the way. What was most painful was the degree of concentration required. Concentration involves shutting out the rest of the world and focusing on one thing. For most of us, that effort is extremely painful. It certainly was for Jeffrey. By using the Reversal of Desire to face that pain, he was able to commit the time and energy he needed to start the writing career he really wanted to have.

The Reversal of Desire gives you a new perspective on family dynamics that have been in place since childhood. *Try the following: Pick something that you got into the habit of avoiding as a child. What was the specific nature of the pain you were avoiding? Now, close your eyes, project yourself into that child, and use the Reversal of Desire on that pain. Imagine yourself as a child using that tool—automatically, every time you want to avoid, day after day, year after year. See if you get a sense of how your life might be different today—not the outward circumstances, but inside yourself. How does it feel different to be you?*

From an early age, Juanita's mother would express disappointment when Juanita did something her mother disapproved of. Juanita's fear of this disapproval kept her from sharing parts of herself that would disappoint her mother. As a result, her mother never really knew her. By using the above exercise, Juanita saw that if she'd pushed through the pain of revealing herself, she would have stopped hiding parts of herself. This, in turn, would have given her mother the opportunity to accept her, and freed her mother to express her real love for every part of her daughter.

SUMMARY OF THE REVERSAL OF DESIRE

What the Tool Is For

Use the tool when you need to take an action you've been avoiding. We avoid doing the things that are most painful for us, preferring to live in a Comfort Zone that severely limits what we get out of life. The tool lets you act in the face of pain and helps you get your life moving again.

What You're Fighting Against

Pain avoidance is a powerful habit. You get immediate relief when you defer something painful. The penalty—helpless regret at a life you wasted—won't come until far in the future. This is why most people can't move forward and live life to the fullest.

Cues to Use the Tool

1. The first cue comes when you have to do something uncomfortable and you feel fear or resistance. Use the tool right before you act.
2. The second cue occurs whenever you *think* about doing something painful or difficult. If you use the tool every time you have these thoughts, you'll build a force that will allow you to act when the time comes.

The Tool in Brief

1. Focus on the pain you're avoiding; see it appear in front

of you as a cloud. Silently scream, "Bring it on!" to demand the pain; you want it because it has great value.

2. Scream silently, "I love pain!" as you keep moving forward. Move so deeply into the pain you're at one with it.

3. Feel the cloud spit you out and close behind you. Say inwardly, "Pain sets me free!" As you leave the cloud, feel yourself propelled forward into a realm of pure light.

The Higher Force You're Using

The higher force that drives all of life expresses itself in relentless Forward Motion. The only way to connect to this force is to be in forward motion yourself. But to do that, you must face pain and be able to move past it. The Reversal of Desire lets you do this. Once the tool connects you to the Force of Forward Motion, the world is less intimidating, your energy is greater, and the future seems more hopeful.

CHAPTER 3

The Tool:
Active Love

The Higher Force:
Outflow

IT WAS MY FIRST SESSION WITH AMANDA, AN AM-bitious, sharply dressed woman in her twenties who entered my office with the force of an invading army. She was having a problem with her boyfriend and demanded an immediate solution. "We were at this party, and he didn't, like, look at me or talk to me the entire evening. He spent the whole time in a cozy little corner flirting with this girl who works at the *cosmetics counter at Macy's.* What world is he living in that he thinks he can get away with that?" she spat out contemptuously.

An electronic rendition of "Someone Like You" interrupted us. Amanda whipped out her phone and barked, "Can't talk now—in a meeting," and without missing a beat, turned back to me and continued. "Let me explain:

I'm starting a company designing and manufacturing high-end women's clothing, and we're in a do-or-die phase where we either attract a lot of money or I go back to waitressing," she said, turning up her nose. "Every night there's another meeting with potential backers. Blake—that's my boyfriend—Blake knows he has to come, and it's his job to make me look good, not to humiliate me with some bimbo!"

To my surprise, as we explored their relationship, it soon became clear that in many ways Blake was the perfect partner for Amanda. Strikingly handsome and refined, he "showed" well in public. And because he wasn't part of the fashion scene (he was a medical researcher), his ego wasn't involved in her career. He was gracious in the face of her moody, imperious style. In fact, he fit her needs so well, she'd insisted they move in together soon after they met.

"It sounds like there's a lot going for the relationship," I ventured.

"Of course there is. I've worked longer on this relationship than I ever have before."

"Really? How long have you been together?"

"Four months." I started to laugh and then realized she wasn't joking. She shot back defensively, "The fashion industry isn't easy on relationships."

The problem wasn't the industry—it was Amanda. A person who invaded my office like General Patton's army was going to have trouble with relationships. Unfortunately, this was lost on her.

I tried to say it as gently as I could: "Do you think there's a pattern repeating itself in your relationships that makes them end so quickly?"

"I don't care about patterns," Amanda snapped. "My friend who's a patient of yours promised me you wouldn't waste time talking about the past. All I want you to do is help me get my boyfriend back under control."

I tried to keep the smile off my face. "I can help you, but not by getting anybody under control. . . . But let's put that aside for a moment. Why don't you tell me what happened next."

It turns out that on the car ride back from the party Amanda had given Blake a dressing-down befitting a lowly servant. But this time instead of deferring, Blake had politely stood up to her. "It's already a sacrifice for me to go to these boring events. I only go because you like me there. So for once in our relationship I got off your leash and had a good time, and you're going to beat me up for that?"

Amanda was stunned. The rest of the car ride was silent, but her mind was on fire. Again and again she went over how badly he'd treated her. Like a broken record, she kept telling herself, I'm putting my ass on the line, building a business for us in the most high-pressure industry there is. Can't he make me feel like a woman in this one instance? She began to fantasize revenge. She saw herself sleeping with a GQ model she knew and having Blake discover them just as they climaxed. By the time they got home, she was exhausted, but the thoughts continued as if they had a life of their own. She stayed up all night, her mind churning.

In the morning, Blake did his best to lighten things up. He surprised her with breakfast in bed, complete with fresh-cut flowers. But Amanda would have none of it. Not only wouldn't she talk to him, she wouldn't even look at him. If anything, the hateful thoughts of the night before were even stronger. They now included a litany of his imperfections, even tiny ones like the way he cleared his throat. All of this began to have a physical effect on her. "When he was near me, my skin would crawl. I couldn't stand to be in the same room with him."

"Have you ever had such an extreme reaction with other boyfriends?" I asked.

She looked up. "Only when they deserved it."

"How frequent was that?"

Amanda burst into tears. It turned out that every relationship had ended this way. The guy would do something that set her off the way Blake had. She shrugged her shoulders. "I can't love the person after that. My friend calls it the 'point of no return.'"

THE MAZE

What Blake did was hurtful; maybe he even did it on purpose. But things like that happen to every couple. In a healthy relationship, something like this can be worked out. The real problem here was Amanda's reaction—she withdrew into an unforgiving state that made reconciliation impossible. From then on, Blake wasn't damaging the relationship, she was. She had done this over and over again, driving away even the most accommodating of guys.

There are different versions of the state Amanda got into. She withdrew; others explode or go into attack mode. But the underlying problem is the same: you're so trapped in hurt and anger that you can't move on.

Everyone gets into this state, even people who think of themselves as calm and rational. All it takes is the right stimulus. It might be triggered by someone close to you, who can hurt you with a look or a negative tone. But it could just as easily be a neighbor's loud music or a friend's political opinions.

We call this state "the Maze." It's called the Maze because the deeper you get into it, the harder it is to escape. The person who has "wronged" you becomes your obsession. It's as if they've taken up residence in your head and you can't get them out. You curse them, you argue with them, you plot revenge. In this state, the other person becomes your jailor, trapping you in a maze of your own repetitive thoughts.

Take a moment right now and choose a person who triggers this state in you. Then try this exercise:

> Close your eyes and visualize the other person
> provoking you. React to this intensely, as if it's really
> happening. What are you thinking, and how does it
> make you feel? Note to yourself that this is a distinct
> state of mind.

You may be justified in reacting the way you do—*but it doesn't matter.*

Once you're in the Maze, you're damaging yourself. For Amanda, the damage to her personal life was obvious. If she couldn't get over a minor incident at a party with her boyfriend, there was no hope she could work through the larger problems inevitable in every relationship—which is why hers ended so quickly. How would she ever get married and have children if she couldn't get past the first big fight?

But the Maze is a threat to all relationships, not just marriage, because it warps your view of people. When you're in the Maze, you literally forget everything good about the other person—all you can think about is the wrong he's committed. Objectively, Blake was one of the best guys Amanda had ever met. But once she was in the Maze, there was nothing good about him; even the way he cleared his throat made her want to scream.

That same loss of perspective had also spoiled some of her work relationships. Amanda had lost her temper at a buyer for an upscale department store who was interested in her line of clothing. He retaliated by placing an order with her closest competitor. Amanda was immediately filled with anxious visions of counting tips at a luncheonette. A fall back into waitressing was a fate worse than death, so she'd spent the past few months eating crow, offering inducements for him to come back. Once again, the damage was self-inflicted.

The Maze doesn't just damage your relationship to other people; it damages your relationship to life itself.

When you're in the Maze, life passes you by.

Most wrongs that people commit cause no lasting damage; if you were to let go of the initial hurt, you could go on with life immediately. But you don't. You obsess about what was done to you in the past. As a result, you turn your back on your own future.

A classic example is the adult who still blames her parents for wrecking her life. She entered the Maze long ago and never got out, giving herself a ready excuse to quit on anything that's difficult. She can't write a book because her parents never recognized her talent. She refuses to date, blaming her shyness on an unloving father.

These are examples of how the Maze damages you over a lifetime. There are also short-term examples. Amanda was the godmother of a friend's daughter. She and the friend had a small disagreement, which ended with Amanda deeply in the Maze. As usual, she cut off all contact with her friend. After a few months, Amanda found out she'd missed her goddaughter's first birthday. "That's something I'll regret for the rest of my life," she said.

As a therapist, I've witnessed the toll taken by the Maze; countless hours wasted, rich opportunities lost, *an enormous amount of life that hasn't been lived.*

The most frustrating thing about the Maze is that even after someone can see what it's cost them, they still find it impossible to escape. Amanda was no exception. After a few sessions, she realized she was her own worst enemy. But that realization didn't help her regain control of her mind. The rage, revenge fantasies, and hurt feelings had a momentum of their own. "I reach the point where I can't stand my own thoughts anymore. I can stop them for a second. But then I remember Blake accusing me of being controlling, and it all starts up again."

FAIRNESS

Why is it so hard to get out of the Maze?

We're trapped because of a universal human expectation that the world will treat us fairly. This is a cherished, childish assumption—"If I'm good, the world will be good to me." We should know better—the world violates this assumption every day. Someone cuts you off on the highway, a customer is rude to you. But despite this overwhelming evidence, we cling to our childish views.

As long as you insist that life treat you fairly, when

someone wrongs you you'll demand that the scales of justice be balanced immediately. You'll dig in your heels and refuse to budge until this happens. This is why the Maze almost always involves fantasies of revenge or restitution. You're engaged in a futile attempt to restore fairness to your world.

Most of the time you're unaware of this expectation that people will treat you fairly. But it's there, in the background—which means that, at any moment, you're standing right outside the mouth of the Maze, primed and ready to be swallowed up. All it takes is some injustice—any injustice—and before you have time to think, you're trapped and can't get out.

THE HIGHER FORCE: OUTFLOW

It's not easy to give up your childish expectation of fairness. In my experience, it's only when you feel something bigger, better, and more powerful than fairness that you stop waiting for it. I first experienced this by accident when I was a small child.

I was about five years old and my parents took my older sister and me to the snow, which should have been exciting for someone living in sunny Southern California. But somehow my father hurt my feelings in the car on the way—I can't remember how. What I do remember is that I went into the Maze. I sat in the backseat behind my father and burned holes in the back of his head with my eyes. I wished every possible torture on him. If hatred were flammable, his head would've exploded.

When we arrived at the snow, my family piled out of the car but I refused to budge. I folded my arms across my chest and sat there. My mother tried gentle persuasion. My sister sledded down the hill a couple of times and came back to tell me how fun it was. Even my dad tried to tempt me out of the car. But the harder they tried to persuade me, the more I dug in my heels.

Eventually, they gave up. That's when the strangest thing happened. I glanced outside the car and saw a little puppy sniffing around, lost and shivering in the parking lot. Before I had time to think, I opened the car door, rushed out to gather him in my arms, and brought him back inside the warm car with me. He licked my face. Suddenly everything changed. I was overwhelmed with love for that helpless, scared puppy. I felt my heart unclench, expand. Everything felt so different; it was as if the universe had suddenly tilted on its axis. I didn't hate my father—I loved him, even wanted to be like him: he had taught me to be protective of animals. And that stubborn, cranky, bratty feeling that had possessed me was gone. I felt more grown up—as though I was better than all that petty childishness.

I rushed out of the car and called for my dad. He

came and helped me find the dog's owner, and he told me how proud he was of me. I'm still amazed at how abruptly everything changed. My family cheered for me as I sledded down the hill. I was crying and laughing at the same time. I felt like I'd broken out of prison. All the way home I was singing and laughing. I even managed a kind of inarticulate, five-year-old apology for the jerk I'd been.

Even as a child, I sensed that this incident was about more than my love for the puppy. I'd had an overwhelming experience of a higher force, so powerful it carried me out of the Maze, beyond my petty hurt feelings and stubborn rage. I felt a powerful wave of love for everything and everyone—it gave me the strength to overcome my injured pride and anger.

I had experienced something that was completely different from what we normally call "love." Most of us think of love in its lower form. You feel this type of love only when the other person is pleasing you. You feel it for your child when he smiles at you adoringly; or your partner when she looks particularly attractive. This form of love is weak because it's a reaction to outer circumstances.

The trick to getting out of the Maze is to generate a form of love that's independent of your immediate reactions. After all, your reactions put you in the Maze in the first place.

That's what I experienced when I was five years old. It was bigger than my personal reactions, bigger than me. That's love in its higher form. We have a name for this kind of love: "Outflow."

Outflow is an infinite, spiritual force that gives of itself without restraint. It's like sunlight, shining equally on everything and everyone. The moment you feel this force, you're lifted above your petty hurt feelings. You no longer need a remedy from the offending person because Outflow is its own reward. Unlike fairness, it's a reward that has real value. It lets you go on with your life.

Please be clear: tapping into Outflow doesn't mean giving in or being passive in the face of wrongdoing. We're not counseling that you roll over and let people mistreat you. Outflow changes your *inner* state; in an *outer* sense you're still free to respond however you want to. In fact, you'll find that by tapping into this higher force, you'll be free to be *more aggressive* should you choose to confront someone. As long as you're in the Maze, you still need something from the person who wronged you. This gives that person an intimidating power over you. In Outflow, connected to a higher force, there's no one to be afraid of.

THE TOOL: ACTIVE LOVE

Think of Outflow as a huge tidal wave of bountiful energy, bestowing itself on the world. Although it surrounds you at all times, you can't perceive it until you're in a giving state yourself. You have to be in sync with Outflow just like a surfer has to be in sync with a wave he wants to ride. When you give from the heart, you let yourself be carried by Outflow the same way a surfer does when he paddles forward to catch a wave.

The trick is putting yourself in that state whenever you choose, especially when you're so hurt or angry it feels impossible. At those times, you can't wait passively for something to open your heart, like the puppy did when I was five years old. You have to make a conscious effort to generate love when someone has just wronged you. For most of us this feels unnatural. Like children, we expect love to be effortless. Part of growing up spiritually is understanding that it takes work to be truly loving.

For most of us it's not natural to work at love—we need a tool. The tool is called "Active Love" exactly because it combines love and effort. The work you do when you use the tool creates a miniature flow of love inside you. That puts you in sync with a larger, universal wave of cosmic Outflow.

You should use Active Love whenever someone incites, enrages, or otherwise provokes you to enter the Maze. It's a reliable way of tapping into Outflow. You'll now have the power to free yourself from the Maze in any circumstances. No one will be able to put your life on hold.

Read through the tool before you attempt to use it. It has three steps.

Active Love

Imagine that you're surrounded by a warm, liquid light that is infinitely loving. Feel your heart expand far beyond you to become one with this love. As you bring your heart back to normal size, this infinite energy concentrates itself inside your chest. It's an unstoppably loving force that wants to give itself away.

Focus on the person who's triggered your anger. If they're not physically in front of you (usually they're not) then visualize their presence. Send all the love in your chest directly to them; hold nothing back. It's like completely expelling a deep breath.

Follow the love as it leaves your chest. When it enters the other person at their solar plexus, don't just watch. *Feel* it enter. This will give you the sense you're completely at one with them. Now relax—you'll feel yourself again surrounded by infinite love, which will return to you all the energy you gave away. You'll feel filled up and at peace.

Each of the three steps has a name to help you remember it.

The first step is called "concentration." You're gathering up all the love that surrounds you and concentrating it in your heart—which is the only organ that can find it and hold it.

The second step is called "transmission." In this step your heart functions as a conduit, transmitting love from a higher place into this world.

The real power of the tool is in the third step, which is called "penetration." When you *feel* the love you're transmitting enter the other person, there's a sense of total acceptance; an acceptance that comes only with the experience of oneness. This is a victory—you've embraced injustice completely and are free to move on from it. With this new power, no one has the power to put you in the Maze. No one can stop you.

This ability to be free of the effect of others even applies when you don't know who the other person is. The classic example of this is when somebody cuts you off on the freeway and you can't identify who he is. It also applies to whole organizations, like the post office or the Department of Motor Vehicles. The beauty of the tool is that you need not know who you're angry at—you're using the tool for yourself. It takes nothing away from the power of the tool if you have to imagine what the person or persons look like. You'll probably find yourself doing it naturally. What matters is that you have a figure, real or imagined, to pour your love into. It's that act that sets you free.

Now that you know the tool, every time you feel wronged, you're presented with a choice. You can do nothing and fall back into the Maze where you're trapped in the past. Life will pass you by. Or you can use Active Love, unify yourself with Outflow, and move on with your life. In the initial shock of being mistreated, we all forget that we have this choice. The picture below will help you remember.

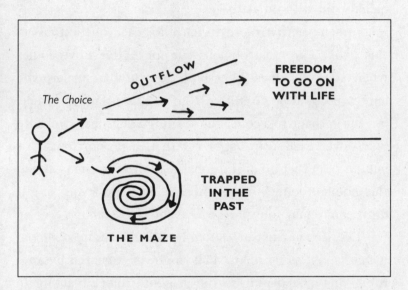

The stick figure is you, the moment after you've experienced an injustice. The lower arrow indicates that you do nothing; in effect, you've chosen to enter the Maze. The upper arrow indicates that you've chosen to put yourself through the three steps of Active Love. This decision unites you with Outflow; you're free to move into the future. Many patients visualize this picture when injured to remind themselves they do have a choice.

HOW TO USE ACTIVE LOVE

Practice the three steps right now—concentration, transmission, penetration. Go through them over and over again so that you can use the tool from memory. You should get to the point where you can run through the three steps quickly but with intensity.

Remember that there are cues for each of the tools in this book. The most obvious cue for Active Love comes when someone does something to you that makes you angry: it could be anything from your son failing to take out the garbage to a colleague stealing your idea. Typically, you'll overreact. Your anger is either disproportionate, or you just can't let go of it; probably both. The cue is anger: the moment you feel it, use Active Love and keep using it until you regain your perspective and move on.

The second cue relates to a less-obvious kind of anger, which is just as frequent. This anger isn't caused by anything that's happening in the present. You're reacting to the memory of something done to you weeks or years ago. If you allow a memory to put you in the Maze, that's just as damaging as being put there by something that just happened. We all have a powerful tendency to ruminate on past injustices. In the midst of an otherwise great day, you'll find yourself remembering someone who snubbed you at a wedding or a colleague who tried to undermine you with your boss. It's at that moment you have to use Active Love.

Finally, Active Love can be used as a way of preparing yourself to deal with difficult people. Each of us knows at least one or two people who are so offensive we go into the Maze at the very thought of them. The classic figure from comedy is the mother-in-law, but it could be your spouse, your child, or your boss. When we anticipate run-ins with these people, we waste a lot of time worrying about how they'll treat us and how we'll react. This doesn't prepare us for the interaction, it's just another version of the Maze.

The only real way to prepare yourself for these encounters is to use Active Love. In fact, you should use it whenever you think of these difficult people. As a result, they'll take up less space in your head. Once you can get out of the Maze at will, they won't have so much power over you and you'll deal with them much more confidently.

If you use these three cues faithfully, you'll find yourself living with less hurt, resentment, and anger, and you'll be free of the people who've always been able to push your buttons.

I should warn you: it isn't always easy to get yourself to use Active Love. When you're in a self-righteous rage, it feels like you *shouldn't* send love to the person who put you in that state. Usually, we think of love in a moralistic or religious context; we try to be loving because it's the "right" thing to do. But the abstract concept of "doing the right thing" isn't enough to change your behavior when you feel wronged. Amanda put it this way: "If you screw with me, I'm going to screw you back. I'm not Gandhi, I'm in the garment industry."

I never ask patients to use Active Love because it's the right thing to do. I tell them to use it because it's in their self-interest. I remind them that they don't want to live in a state of rage—ever; not because it's bad, but because it's painful and debilitating. Morality is important. But there are always times when it isn't strong enough to motivate us. At those times, you have to find something that acts as a more powerful motivator: your own self-interest.

The other reason it's difficult to use Active Love is that anger is such a *reactive* emotion—just seeing the other person's face, even in your imagination, can reinforce your rage and make it impossible to generate love. If you find this happening to you, try this simple technique: when you use the tool, see the other person without a face. A face is the most identifiable aspect of a person. A body without a face could belong to anyone. When you penetrate the person with love, see only his trunk and aim the energy right at his solar plexus. This takes the focus off the other person and puts it back on your task, which is to generate Outflow.

When your goal is generating Outflow, no matter what the circumstances, it helps to think of it as a substance, like water. If you work at a car wash, your job is to hose down each car completely. It doesn't matter whether the car belongs to a saint or your worst enemy—your job is to spray water on each car equally.

But you'll find working with this higher form of love more rewarding than working with any other substance. When you give away love, you end up with more than you had when you began. Unlike water, if your glass is half-filled with love and you give it to your enemy to drink, the glass will return to you full. That's the reason you feel filled up and at peace in the final step of Active Love.

FREQUENTLY ASKED QUESTIONS

By far, the most common objection we hear to using the tools in this book is that they require a lot of work. We discussed this in Chapter 1, but it bears repeating here. We understand that, when you're stressed out, the last thing you want to hear is that there's *something else* you have to do.

But remember: when you use the tools, you're rewarded with much more energy than you put in. There's only one explanation for this: the tools allow you to experience the infinite energy of higher forces. Active Love gives you a good example of this. You give away all your energy, but when you're finished, you have more than you started with. That's why your half-filled glass is always returned full. This is an immediate experience of the infinite.

To reiterate: as human beings we are given access to the infinite, but we have to work for it; it doesn't come for free.

Here are some of the questions people ask about Active Love:

1. Doesn't using Active Love let the other person get away with disrespecting me?

Our natural reaction when we feel disrespected is to confront the other person. Unfortunately, we're usually in the Maze when we do this. Confronting someone when we're enraged never inspires respect; it arouses anger and fear, but not respect. (If you doubt this, just imagine someone venting their wrath on *you* and see what it provokes in you.)

People are more perceptive than you think: when you confront them, they will intuit what you're feeling inside— love or hate—because that tells them how you value the relationship. Conveying hatred says the relationship means nothing to you; you're willing to destroy it. That's why your hate so readily arouses hate in the other person. This happens even when you're in a position of authority and have to supervise other employees. Intimidating or abusing them doesn't inspire their loyalty.

A great communicator has faith that there's a reserve of goodwill in most relationships, even if it's temporarily absent. The only way to activate that potential goodwill is to be in an Outflow state before you confront somebody. This sends the signal that you still value the relationship. Once the other person feels this, they become much more likely to take in what you're saying and respond respectfully. Once in a while, Active Love won't work because the other person has no goodwill. You've lost nothing, because you never would've gained this person's respect in any case. In fact, you'll feel a kind of calm confidence rather than the raw, obsessive emotions that overwhelmed you in the Maze because you'll see the other person with clarity.

For most people, Active Love creates a new model of confrontation. Use the tool *before* you say anything to the other person, even before you're in his presence; keep using it until you can feel yourself go into an Outflow state. Once you're in this state, you're ready to confront the other person. It will allow you to be assertive without being provocative.

It may seem strange to use love as a preparation for confrontation. Try it with an open mind and observe what really happens.

2. I don't want to use Active Love because it's a lie. Isn't it fake to send love to someone you actually hate?

Psychology has trained us to think that we should communicate all of our feelings honestly because emotions represent "the truth" of a situation. This is a fallacy. Emotions represent only a slice of the truth. Take Amanda and Blake: she truly hated him when he allowed another woman to monopolize his attention at the dinner party. But before the dinner party, she loved him. So to say that her hatred represented the whole truth of their relationship—the intricately woven fabric of their life together—is an absurd oversimplification. The "truth" is always multifaceted.

You've probably had the experience of looking back on a fight and been amazed that you got so worked up over something that now seems laughably unimportant. In a moment of rage, you think all kinds of things that seem "true" but really just reflect how angry you are at that moment. To express or act on that "truth" is insane; no relationship could ever survive this rigid, literal kind of "honesty."

It's a waste of time thinking you know the ultimate truth about another person. All you get is the sense that you're "right"; the ultimate booby prize. The only thing that will really help you is to develop the power to reshape the relationship in a positive way. You can't do this as long as you're caught up in your immediate reactions; Active Love gives you the power to transcend them.

This is the real power of a spiritual approach to psychology. It teaches you how to activate higher forces, which are stronger than your emotions. These forces won't replace your emotions, but they will transform them. As you stop wasting energy on superficial annoyances the important things in life will move you more deeply.

3. In step one of the tool, I can't get myself to believe that the world of love exists. What should I do?

You aren't aware of it, but you actually *resist* feeling that world of love. You resist it because it's so powerful. The human ego doesn't like to experience anything more powerful than itself.

You can get around this by focusing on your heart, which has no need to aggrandize itself. Imagine you have a strong sense of needy vulnerability in your heart, almost as if your heart were begging. Direct your sense of need toward this world of love. The more deeply you can feel this need, the more real the world of love will become.

Taking a second to open your heart like this prepares you to use the tool. As you practice, your heart will soften and it will become a powerful channel for higher forces.

At first, it will feel strange to stay vulnerable in a hostile situation. Work up to this by putting yourself in that state when you're alone. Like any other skill, this takes practice. That's why a baseball player spends time in a batting cage before he goes up against a live pitcher.

The more committed you are to this vulnerable state, the more power you'll feel. This comes as a shock to most people. That's because they don't understand what real power is. Real power doesn't come from you as an individual. It comes from the fact that you're channeling something greater than you.

When you have real power, you have no need to prove anything to anyone. Free of your own ego, you're functioning from the highest part of yourself. In this state, you can inspire the higher parts of those around you. That's the only way conflict is truly resolved.

OTHER USES OF ACTIVE LOVE

What if you're not like Amanda? Can Active Love still help you?

It can, because like all the other tools in this book, Active Love has a much broader application than can be presented with one patient. Below I describe three patients who are different from Amanda and who used Active Love in novel situations. In each case, it enabled the patient to develop a strength he or she didn't have before.

Active Love builds self-control. *Nothing is more destructive for you and those around you than a temper you can't control. The only way to rein this in is to have a tool that works right in the moment, defusing the bomb before it explodes.*

Ray's explosions mostly happened in public places. If someone bumped him on the sidewalk or cut him off in his car, he was ready to go. But because he had no other definition of manhood, when he felt dissed, he was in the middle of a fight before he could think. At age forty, he was still fighting strangers in the streets. His problem came to a head when two young guys in a car blocked him from getting on the highway. They drove off laughing, but he tailgated them for miles, bumping them from behind. When he followed them down an exit ramp, they got out of their car with bats. This incident was a turning point for Ray. "I knew I was getting too old to fight for respect from every young punk," he said.

Thinking would never be the answer for his problem. Ray needed a tool that worked at the moment he felt provoked. I taught him to use Active Love at those moments. Not only did it allow him to control himself, it did something more profound. It gave him the experience of real manhood. "Every time I don't lose it, I respect myself more. The punks can think whatever they want."

Active Love lets you be more assertive. *Nothing is more frustrating than being angry at someone and feeling unable to express it. The more the anger builds up, the more dangerous the confrontation seems. A tool that defuses your anger makes it safe for you to assert yourself.*

Marcy had worked in the billing department of a law firm for years. The department was run by Al, an accountant twenty years older than Marcy. Marcy had no college degree but was the brightest, most reliable employee he had. Although she was his go-to person when there was a problem, he was brusque and dismissive of her the rest of the time. Marcy was too passive to speak up for herself. But after three years without a raise, she was seething inside, filled with fantasies about how she'd tell him off. That made him seem even more intimidating.

I asked her to use Active Love every time she was

around him. To her shock, this made him seem less intimidating, more human. She finally reached the point where she was able to confront him. In an Outflow state, she was able to speak calmly and with self-respect. She got the raise she deserved.

Active Love trains you to accept others as they are. *Everyone in your life is imperfect, either because of something they've done in the past or something they can't change in the present. Fixating on these things destroys relationships. You need a tool that allows you to accept people despite their flaws.*

Mark wanted to marry his girlfriend, but he couldn't get over her past. Long before he met her, she'd had a relationship with a wannabe rock star. She was twenty-three years old, had had little life experience, and thought he was cool. He pulled her into his sex-drugs-and-rock-and-roll lifestyle. She'd had enough after six months and walked out. But Mark couldn't let go of it. He was offended that she'd had sex with a guy who was a notorious womanizer, but the fact that she used drugs with him was even worse. He viewed her as somehow contaminated by the experience, as if she had a stain on her that could never be removed. A phone call from someone who knew her ex-boyfriend, an old photograph, or even a song was enough to set off his Maze-like obsession about what his girlfriend and this guy had done together. His imagination would run wild and he'd interrogate her about the relationship, trying to trick her into inconsistencies. What really bothered him was that whatever had happened was irrevocable. There was no way to restore her purity.

His only alternative was to train himself to accept her. He used Active Love the moment his obsession restarted. That weakened the hold her past had over him. He learned to trust her for the person she had actually become in the present.

SUMMARY OF ACTIVE LOVE

What the Tool Is For

When someone enrages you and you can't get the person out of your head. You may replay what he or she did or fantasize about getting revenge. This is the Maze. It puts your life on hold while the world moves forward without you.

What You're Fighting Against

The childish belief that people will treat you "fairly." You refuse to move forward with life until the wrong you experienced is rectified. Since that rarely happens, you're trapped.

Cues to Use the Tool

1. Use Active Love the moment someone does something that angers you.
2. Use it when you find yourself reliving a personal injustice whether it was in the recent or distant past.
3. Use it to prepare yourself to confront a difficult person.

The Tool in Brief

1. Concentration: Feel your heart expand to encompass the world of infinite love surrounding you. When your heart contracts back to normal size, it concentrates all this love inside your chest.
2. Transmission: Send all the love from your chest to the other person, holding nothing back.

3. Penetration: When the love enters the other person, don't just watch, *feel* it enter; sense a oneness with him or her. Then relax, and you'll feel all the energy you gave away returned to you.

The Higher Force You're Using

Active Love creates Outflow. Outflow is the force that accepts everything as it is. This dissolves your sense of unfairness so you can give without reservation. Once you're in that state, nothing can make you withdraw. You are the chief beneficiary; you become unstoppable.

CHAPTER 4

The Tool:
Inner Authority

The Higher Force:
The Force of Self-Expression

THE SON OF A PATIENT OF MINE HAD JUST BEEN accepted by an elite soccer team. This was big news in the West L.A. neighborhood where they lived. My patient, Jennifer, was a huge supporter of her son's athletic career. Ordinarily tentative and unsure of herself, on this occasion Jennifer had done everything she could think of to influence the coach's decision. She spoke to him a number of times, exchanged e-mails with a local sportswriter, and approached anyone else who might have some say. All this effort was for the privilege of driving to obscure parts of Southern California to sit in the blazing heat and watch a game whose intricacies she couldn't grasp. Her son was ten years old.

Jennifer had grown up in a small rural town, the first in

her family to graduate from high school. As soon as she could, she escaped to the big city, using her striking beauty to get a job as a model. But on the inside, she never fully escaped. Despite some success, she couldn't shake the feeling that the people in her upscale neighborhood were better than she was—smarter, more sophisticated, more secure. In her imagination, they were members of an in-group she could never join.

She was bound and determined that her son would never feel excluded the way she did. Unlike her, he would go to college—not just any college, but a first-rate institution, preferably in the Ivy League. Club soccer was only the first step in this crusade to storm the bastions of legitimacy. From there, he'd get into a prep school, a select college, and voilà—he'd be admitted into the in-group.

Jennifer's father, who still lived in the same small town, was offended by her master plan. To him, it reeked of elitism. "My grandson's going to end up drinking white wine instead of Budweiser." Her response was "As long as it's expensive white wine."

Needless to say, when the coach called with his acceptance, Jennifer was overjoyed. But the thrill didn't last long. From the first day of practice, Jennifer felt like an outsider. A lot of the other boys had fathers who were successful lawyers and businessmen. Her son's father was a loser who'd abandoned her as soon as she became pregnant. The other fathers coached their sons on such subtleties as slide tackles, penalty kicks, and offside rules. Jennifer couldn't remember what the yellow and red cards were for.

But the moms were even worse. When Jennifer would arrive at a practice, she'd see them bunched together in breathless conversation. Sometimes she'd catch them giving her strange looks. Not once did they make room for her to sit with them. "They'll never accept me. They already think I'm trash," Jennifer told me.

"How do you know what they're thinking?" I asked. "Have you ever even spoken to them?" I encouraged her to reach out to them. The next week there was a parents' meeting to plan transportation to the next set of road games. Against her better judgment, Jennifer forced herself to attend. It didn't go well. "I wanted to introduce myself, but each time I came up to someone, I froze. . . . My mouth dried up, my voice got all shaky. I sounded like such a freak. I got out of there as fast as I could."

Everyone has moments like this; you want to make a good impression but your brain and body betray you. We call these moments of "freezing." Jennifer's symptoms were typical—dry mouth, shakiness, and "brain lock," an inability to remember information or even form coherent sentences. Sometimes people lose an accurate sense of their bodies, accidentally spilling or bumping into things. Moments of freezing can range from mild, in which the person feels an uncomfortable stiffness, to extreme, in which the person literally can't move or speak, the proverbial deer caught in headlights.

All of us have experienced some type of freezing. It's common to think it happens in front of a large group, but frequently it can be one person who makes you freeze—say, your boss or your mother-in-law. In this chapter, when we use the word *audience*, it doesn't necessarily mean a group of people; even one person can qualify. *Audience* just means someone whose opinion of you is important at any given moment.

It's also common to think that we freeze because of the situation we're in—meeting an intimidating person or speaking to a large group. But freezing is actually caused by an inner insecurity; an insecurity you may not even be aware of until you suddenly lose your ability to express yourself.

Let's see how this works in your life:

> Close your eyes and imagine yourself in front of a person or group who makes you feel insecure. Focus on your body. Identify any of the symptoms of freezing we've mentioned. What is it like to try to express yourself in the face of these symptoms?

If you're like most people, it is awkward and uncomfortable. But a little awkwardness wouldn't matter if it were the only price you paid for insecurity. Unfortunately, it costs a lot more than that.

THE PRICE OF INSECURITY

Insecurity destroys people's ability to connect with one another. Over time, insecurity makes you stiff and uninteresting to other people, and, paradoxically, it also makes you ungiving. Insecure people are so obsessed with how others perceive them that they give almost nothing of themselves. As a result, they feel even more alienated.

What happened to Jennifer was a perfect example of this. After the parents' meeting, she no longer had any doubts that everyone despised her. Soccer practice became torture; in her imagination, she was now persona non grata. She walked to her lonely place at the top bleacher like an inmate to the electric chair, with her eyes averted and her heart pounding. She became obsessed with various schemes to get the other parents to accept her. One week, she declared triumphantly, "I found the answer. It's my accent! There are still traces of my old twang. I already have an appointment with a speech coach."

Happily, before she wasted a lot of time and money, fate intervened. The team chartered a bus for their first away game. With her son contentedly chattering away with his buddies in the back of the bus, Jennifer bravely leaned forward and struck up a conversation with some mothers sitting in front of her. They seemed wary at first, but eventually they warmed up to her and admitted the truth. At every practice they'd see this perfectly proportioned model march confidently past them—in outfits they'd kill to be able to fit into. She wouldn't even deign to say hello. "You seemed completely stuck-up and uninterested in us!"

The parents' meeting only made things worse—it was all they could do to get their husbands to shut up about this sexy single mother who had mysteriously disappeared early in the evening. Some of them were so unnerved, they'd hired personal trainers. They laughed when she admitted she'd hired a speech coach.

It was embarrassing for Jennifer to admit how warped her perspective had become. She had come to see the other parents as a separate and superior race of beings who, in addition to mastering the infinite subtleties of soccer, raised confident, well-behaved children in intact, financially secure families. "Now I realize how crazy that was— most of their lives are a mess."

More important, she realized that she'd become self-obsessed, even withholding. "The truth is, I was unfriendly," she admitted. This caused the other parents to feel insecure about her. To them, she looked like a beautiful female predator who would get everything she wanted, leaving a trail of broken families in her wake.

Insecurity swept through this group of mature, rational adults like an opportunistic infection. Both sides were completely wrong about each other, and until they could connect, neither could see reality clearly. If Jennifer had listened to her insecurity, an entire group of families would have remained shut out of her and her son's life.

Connecting to others is also an essential ingredient in

success. The most important opportunities in life come from other people. It would be nice if they granted those opportunities based on merit; a reward for talent or hard work. But that's not the way the world works. *People give you opportunities because they feel connected to you.* I know an extreme example of this. My best friend is a world-class theoretical physicist who teaches at a major university and is a member of the prestigious National Academy of Sciences. He has a colleague who is far superior to him in ability, but who has never been nominated for the Academy. Why? Because her insecurities make her competitive, jealous, and hard to work with. Despite her superior ability, she has limited her professional advancement.

Jennifer had her own problems connecting, but for a less obvious reason. Before I met her, she'd tried to move from modeling into acting. She attracted a talent agent quickly, but auditions were another matter. The most important part of any audition is connecting to the people in the room. She memorized her lines perfectly, but her performances were so stilted that those watching were bored. After the umpteenth rejection, her agent fired her. "You work hard and your looks are perfect," he said. "But when you audition, you turn into a robot. Maybe you should see a shrink."

She wasn't ready yet. She figured she could get rid of her insecurity on her own. She went on a campaign not unlike the one that got her son into club soccer. She hired an acting coach. She wrote down all of her aspirations and visualized herself winning an Oscar. This all-out war on her insecurity made her feel better only for a short time. Before long, the negative feeling—"no one likes you"—came back just as strong.

Over and over again, we've seen how hard it is to make insecurity go away. Facts and logic don't work. Insecure people often go to extraordinary lengths for some goal they hope will make them feel better—they'll lose weight, get an advanced degree, work 24–7 to win a promotion. But every time, the sense of inadequacy returns; insecurity seems to have a life of its own.

Why is insecurity so difficult to get rid of?

The answer will seem very strange at first. Inside each of us is a *second self*, a living being we're deeply ashamed of. No matter how hard you try, you can never get rid of this second self.

THE SHADOW

The idea of a second self living inside you may seem unbelievable. Keep an open mind and follow what happened to Jennifer.

Once Jennifer realized that her insecurity was irrational, I asked her to close her eyes. "Go back to the parents' meeting where you froze up; re-create all those shaky feelings you had." She nodded. "Now, push the feelings out in front of you and give them a face and body. This figure is the embodiment of everything you feel insecure about." I paused. "When you're ready, tell me what you see."

There was a long silence. Jennifer flinched suddenly, then blinked her eyes open. "Ugh," she said grimacing. "I saw this thirteen- or fourteen-year-old girl, overweight, unwashed. Her face was pasty and covered with zits . . . a complete loser."

Jennifer had just seen her Shadow.

The "Shadow" is everything we don't want to be but fear we are, represented in a single image. It's called the Shadow because it follows us wherever we go.

The great Swiss psychiatrist Carl Jung was the first to say that everyone has a Shadow regardless of their accomplishments, talents, or appearance. The Shadow is one of many "archetypes" we're born with. An archetype is a patterned way of perceiving the world. For example, everyone is born with a sense of what a mother should be like. Jung would call this the "archetypal" mother. This is an archetype, not to be confused with your real, biological mother. However, this archetype does shape what you expect from your real mother. There are many archetypes—Mother, Father, God, the Devil, to name a few—and each has a profound effect on how you experience the world.

There's a way in which the Shadow is different from all the other archetypes: the others affect how you see the world; *the Shadow determines how you see yourself.* Take Jennifer: to others, she was a beautiful, perfectly proportioned model with flawless hair and makeup. But to herself, she was an ugly stray cat; a social reject. No wonder she felt insecure.

Now you can understand why insecurity is so hard to get rid of. You can eliminate a specific flaw—Jennifer had long ago cleaned up her acne and lost her adolescent pudginess—but you can't eliminate the Shadow itself. It's part of being human.

Let's see what your Shadow looks like.

> Go back to the feeling you had in the last exercise: you're in front of a group of people who make you feel insecure and self-conscious. Focus on the emotions this brings up. Now push those feelings out in front of you and imagine they form a being with a face and body.

You've just seen your Shadow. Make a careful note of what it looks like. Don't worry if you have the "right" image; there isn't one. Everyone's Shadow looks different. But no matter what it looks like, its appearance is unsettling: the handsome ladies' man whose Shadow looked like a lumbering troll; the female CEO of a Fortune 500 company whose Shadow looked like a lonely, weeping eight-year-old girl. It might be unlikable, ugly, or stupid. As you work with it, its appearance may change.

The Shadow is the source of one of the most basic human conflicts. Everyone wants to feel that as an individual we have value. But when we look inside ourselves, we see the Shadow and we're ashamed. Our immediate reaction is to turn away—to look *outside* ourselves for some evidence of our worth. This takes the form of looking to others for approval and validation.

If you doubt how widespread this search for attention is, look at the way we worship celebrity. We think that because celebrities have gained the recognition of the world, they must be happy and secure. Despite repeated rehabs, failed relationships, and public humiliations, we persist in believing that being the center of attention gives them the sense of worth we crave.

The advertising industry spends billions of dollars each year—all of it preying on our need for acceptance. Every advertisement boils down to a simple message: if you buy our product you'll be accepted, loved, part of the in-crowd; if you don't you're stuck . . . alone with your Shadow. This reinforces our belief that self-worth can be acquired in the same way we purchase a house or a car.

The problem is, no amount of approval from others can make you feel worthy—because no amount of validation can eliminate your Shadow. Anytime you're alone and you turn inward—there's your Shadow, making you feel embarrassed and inferior. Phil and I have seen famous patients who are constantly showered with validation and fawned over in the press. This kind of worship doesn't improve their self-worth; it makes them fragile and babyish. They become dependent on attention the way an infant is on a pacifier.

Whether you're a celebrity or not, when you crave the approval of others, you give them power over you. They become authority figures who define your value. Like a Roman emperor, they cast their thumbs up or down in what seems like a final judgment of your worth. No wonder you freeze in their presence.

The picture below shows how this works.

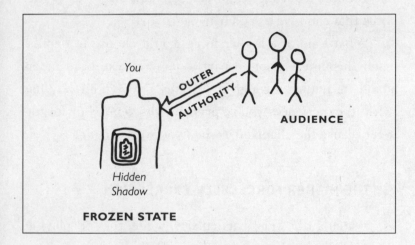

The picture diagrams the state of affairs in someone prone to freezing (which is almost everyone). The person is ashamed of his Shadow and does everything possible to keep it hidden inside him. This is illustrated by the box around the shaded figure labeled "Hidden Shadow." The audience figures in the upper right are big because the person experiences them as having the power to define his value. This power comes at him through the arrows labeled "Outer Authority." Since he's hiding his Shadow, the external force causes him to freeze.

As the picture makes clear, looking outward doesn't work any better than looking inward; either way, a real sense of self-worth tends to elude us.

There is a way to find it; it involves a profound secret. What appears to be a weak and inferior Shadow is really the conduit for a higher force—and it's only this higher force that can give us enduring self-worth.

What kind of a higher force would choose to express itself through a despised part of us? You can best understand its nature through experiences you've already had with it; experiences you've probably discounted or forgotten because they happened when you were a child.

THE HIGHER FORCE: SELF-EXPRESSION

Watch little kids, particularly when they're playing. They aren't self-conscious or insecure. They express themselves freely and exuberantly. *They almost never freeze.*

The reason they don't is that they're filled with a higher force called the "Force of Self-Expression." It has a magical quality: it drives us to reveal ourselves in a truthful, genuine way—without caring at all how other people react. As a consequence, when you're connected to this force, you speak with unusual intensity and clarity.

Everyone has experienced this force at some point in their adult lives—maybe in an excited discussion about something that's personally meaningful, maybe when you're comforting a friend in a crisis, even when you're making up a bedtime story for your kids. In each instance and a thousand others, you've lost yourself in the experience and allowed the Force of Self-Expression to speak through you. You've become a conduit for something wiser and more fluent than your normal self. There's relief and joy in this.

The spoken word isn't the only way the Force of Self-Expression emerges. There's a degree of self-expression in almost every human activity. One example is writing. A patient described it like this: "When I finished my script, I had the feeling I hadn't authored any of it. I'm just not that good. It felt like the whole thing had been dictated to me and I copied it down."

The power even functions without words. When athletes say they're "in the zone," they're really connected to the Force of Self-Expression. Watch a great basketball player make an impossible move. He isn't thinking, Which lane is open? or How tall is the defender? He's stopped thinking, stepped aside, and let this higher force take over. In fact, any human endeavor can provide a place for this force to express itself.

When you're connected to the Force of Self-Expression, a part of you speaks that's usually silent. You're speaking from your deepest, inner self. This inner self has its own authority that's not dependent on the approval of others.

Children naturally speak and act in harmony with this inner self. That's how they're able to express themselves with such abandon.

But as we grow into adults, we turn away from this inner self. All our attention and activity becomes focused on the outside world. We start to look there for approval; by the time we're adolescents, we crave the acceptance of our peers as if it were the Holy Grail.

That creates a new problem: we have to hide anything about ourselves that others might not like. Amazingly, the hiding place becomes our own, inner self. We use it as a garbage bag, dumping everything that's unacceptable about ourselves into it. The inner self is still there, but now it's buried under our worst qualities.

In the process, we've turned something that was beautiful—the inner self—into something we despise: the Shadow. It may seem like the worst part of us, but really, it's the doorway to the inner self. Only when that doorway is open can we truly express ourselves.

But achieving that is not easy when you've hidden your Shadow your whole life; it takes a powerful tool.

THE TOOL: INNER AUTHORITY

There's one big difference between this tool and the two you've already learned. The Reversal of Desire and Active Love evoke higher forces that are independent of the obstacles they overcome. But in the tool you're about to learn, the higher force comes from the obstacle itself. The tool turns the Shadow into a conduit for a higher force—the Force of Self-Expression.

To explain how this process works, you need to understand how Phil discovered the tool:

———

I had decided to present some of the new ideas I was developing at a seminar. I was nervous about it. Speaking to a whole group of strangers in a formal setting is a lot scarier than having a one-on-one session with a patient in the comfort of your office. I had terrifying visions of freezing, blanking on what I wanted to say, or even being unable to speak. To avoid this humiliation, I wrote down every word on little cards—just in case my mind went blank.

The result was a disaster.

Gripping my cards for dear life, I stood stiffly in front of the audience. I read what I'd written in a monotone, glancing up compulsively to gauge what they thought. Nothing could have been worse than the reaction I got—they felt sorry for me. I wanted to jump into a deep hole, but none was available.

After two hours of this torture, there was a break. The audience clustered in small groups, speaking in the hushed tones of mourners after a funeral. They were too embarrassed to approach me. I sat alone onstage, feeling radioactive. I had no idea how I was going to give the second half of the seminar.

Then, at my most despairing moment, the strangest thing happened.

In my mind's eye, I saw a figure approaching me. It felt real. It was a young, skinny version of myself—innocent, fearful, and deeply ashamed. It represented my worst fear; that I'd be seen as an inexperienced, faltering child when I wanted to be seen as an authoritative expert. Despite my reaction, it wouldn't go away; despite its appearance, it stared at me aggressively.

I had the strange sensation it was offering me help. I had no idea why, but I suddenly felt energized. Spontaneously, I stood up and walked eagerly toward the audience. They sensed this and quickly returned to their seats, probably wondering why I had this mad smile on what had been my stone face. Before I knew what I was doing, I threw away my notes, opened my mouth, and for the next two hours, I was seized by a force I'd never felt before. Speaking completely off the cuff, I gave an impassioned presentation of my ideas. Surprisingly, I never once thought about what I was going to say; it came spontaneously out of my mouth. Throughout the presentation, I felt the distinct presence of the Shadow. In fact, it felt like he and I were speaking as a unit.

It ended in a standing ovation.

My intuition had always told me there was something valuable hidden inside the Shadow, but on that day

I experienced it directly. It was when I completely lost hope of impressing the audience that the Shadow appeared—I no longer had to hide it. To my great shock, its appearance didn't destroy the ability to express myself—it enhanced it. No longer concerned with what the audience thought of me, I expressed myself with an authority I'd never known before.

As great as the experience was, it was nothing more than a free introductory offer to the power of the Shadow. I couldn't rely on it to happen by itself again. I set out to find a tool that my patients and I could use to harness the self-expressive power of the Shadow.

The tool is called "Inner Authority." This means just what it says. It's not an authority that comes from the approval of anyone outside you; it's the authority you can get only when you're speaking from your inner self.

In order to use Inner Authority, you need to be able to see an image of your Shadow. You've already seen it once; in the section on the Shadow, you projected your insecure feelings out in front of you until they formed a being you could see. Try doing the same thing again. Don't worry about getting the "right" image; it will continue evolving anyway. What's most important is that you feel a real presence in front of you. Practice conjuring up the Shadow until it becomes easy.

You're going to learn the tool by using an imaginary audience. It doesn't matter if it's an audience of one or a group; it doesn't matter if they're strangers or people you know. The only thing that matters is that it's an audience you feel insecure about addressing. You're going to use the tool to unfreeze yourself because you have something to express.

Inner Authority

Imagine that you're standing in front of an audience of one or many. See an image of your Shadow off to one side, facing you. Ignore the audience completely and focus all of your attention on the Shadow. Feel an unbreakable bond between the two of you—as a unit you're fearless.

Together, you and the Shadow forcefully turn toward the audience and silently command them to "LISTEN!" Feel the authority that comes when you and your Shadow speak with one voice.

Once you've used the tool, it should feel like you've cleared a space where you're free to express yourself. All you have to do is stay focused on the connection to the Shadow. If you don't feel freed up, repeat the tool until it creates a sense of flow.

The tool consists of three steps: projecting the Shadow image, feeling a bond with it, and then silently commanding them to listen as you turn to face the audience. Practice these steps until you can move through them quickly. You want the steps to become second nature, so that you can use them in front of people, even while you're speaking.

As you practice the tool and call up the Shadow, its appearance may change. That's not a bad thing. Like anything else that's alive, the Shadow evolves. What's most important is that its presence forms an unbreakable bond you can feel.

The picture below shows how Inner Authority works.

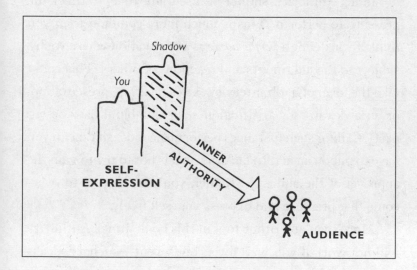

The person in the picture has brought the Shadow out of hiding. It's now outside the person and bonded with him. Speaking with one voice, they evoke the Force of Self-Expression. This higher force gives the person inner authority, indicated by the arrow moving out toward the audience. The figures representing the audience are small and below the person—they're no longer a threat.

The expressive power of the inner self is released through this bond with the Shadow. Once you become an advanced practitioner of the tool, you'll be able to express yourself freely in situations that you would've frozen in previously.

WHEN TO USE INNER AUTHORITY

Inner Authority should be used any time you feel the pressure to perform. This is much more common than you think if you define a *performance* as any situation where you're subject to the judgments and reactions of others. This could take the form of a job interview, sales meeting, presentation, or an awkward social situation such as a blind date or big party. Calling such instances performances doesn't mean you have to put on an act. In fact, the goal is not to try to gain the approval of the audience. Rather, you use the tool to overcome that pressure and express yourself freely.

More than any other tool in this book, Inner Authority will not work if you wait for a "big" event—such as speaking before hundreds of people—to use it for the first time. These events are so intimidating that you'll freeze unless you work up to them. If you practice the tool when you're alone, doing it again and again until it feels like second nature, you'll soon be ready to try it in front of people. Start by using the tool when you're around someone who *doesn't* make you anxious—a family member, a coworker, your best friend, or your spouse. Most of us feel some need for acceptance even around these people.

Now you're ready to tackle situations that cause you anxiety. You might be facing a confrontation or a request for help that you feel uncomfortable making. Push yourself into these situations intentionally and use Inner Authority right in the middle of them. The more you do this, the less intimidated you'll feel.

Once you make Inner Authority a natural part of your daily life, you can start to use it for big events, such as important public speeches. When you use Inner Authority during these intimidating occasions, something amazing will happen: you'll start to look forward to some of them—not because they're stress-free, but because you'll feel excitement at the prospect of expressing yourself.

Learning how to use Inner Authority is like gradually increasing the weights you lift in the gym; it requires a steady buildup. But you also need a cue to remember when to use the tool in your daily life. That ongoing cue is performance anxiety. For Jennifer, that cue obviously meant the soccer practice. At first, she walked over to the bleachers without saying anything to anybody, just using Inner Authority over and over again. That helped her calm down and gradually she was able to speak to the other parents.

But her awareness of performance anxiety also helped her realize that she felt insecure even when she wasn't in front of other people. Thinking about an upcoming blind date, she realized she was anxious, and she used Inner Authority to calm herself. She even started using it in front of the mirror in the morning. "I'm the most judgmental audience I've ever faced," she admitted.

Together with her Shadow, Jennifer began to dispel the insecurity that had plagued her for her entire life.

No one does this in one fell swoop. Sometimes you'll use Inner Authority and you'll immediately relax and express yourself with an ease that feels uncanny. But there will also be situations where the tool will feel mechanical or won't work at all. Don't be discouraged; simply move on to the next cue. The most important thing you can do is to keep connecting to the Shadow without expecting an immediate reward.

Our need to please an audience is a deeply ingrained habit. The best way to break the habit is to replace it with a healthier one; that means using Inner Authority every chance you get. If you do this consistently, you train yourself to rely on your inner self, not on the reactions of others.

Everyone has a place where their need for validation inhibits them, including both of the authors. Psychotherapists are human too, and it's human nature to want our patients to respond to our brilliance. But they don't always do that; in fact, sometimes they look at us as if we're nuts. We'd be lying if we didn't admit that those times are a direct challenge to our own confidence. But it's exactly those moments—when a patient needs to open his mind to a new way of looking at life—that we need to maintain our own sense of authority.

Arguing the point doesn't convey authority—it just reflects our need to be right. What convinces patients is the depth and enthusiasm with which we explain our approach—even when they're challenging us. That can come only from the Force of Self-Expression, which means we have to use Inner Authority just like anyone else would.

THE SECRET BENEFITS OF SELF-EXPRESSION

After Jennifer had been using the tool for a couple of months, something profound happened. I knew it from the way she floated into my office. Instead of staring at the floor, she looked right at me, radiating warmth. "You won't believe the incredible day I had," she said breathlessly. She had started out the day anxious, but this time it had nothing to do with soccer practice. It was triggered by an acting audition, the first she'd had in years. Soon she was sitting tensely with the other actresses in a small waiting room, awaiting her turn.

"As soon as I started reading my lines, I could feel myself freezing up, but I used Inner Authority quickly, twice in a row," she said. "I calmed down, but then I felt something else; like I shifted into another gear." Suddenly she was on her feet, dominating my office as if it were a stage. There was a musical sense of excitement in her voice. "You know how I'm usually so worried about what other people are thinking? It was like I forgot to worry. My lines, the character, my motivation—all of it just came to me without any effort." Overwhelmed by what she'd done, she began to cry softly. That made her even more radiant.

And there was more. After the audition, a friend on the fund-raising committee of her son's school had an emergency and asked if Jennifer could substitute for her at a meeting with an important donor. "I was petrified. But I couldn't say no; she's bailed me out too many times in the past."

Her friend had crammed Jennifer full of financial figures, but as soon as she was introduced to the donor, she couldn't remember anything. So she used Inner Authority a few more times. "I guess I must've really earned the Shadow's trust," she said, "because it was even better than the audition. I just opened my mouth and out came this persuasive pitch. I talked from the heart, about how grateful I was when my son was admitted, how easy it's been for him to make friends and how much he seems to love learning. And when I needed the statistics my friend had prepped me with, they came back to me." Jennifer smiled. "The donor doubled his commitment. They want me to join the fund-raising committee."

For the first time in Jennifer's life, she had a real sense of self. "I felt more myself than I ever have before." She also noticed a strange paradox. "I was speaking with my own voice, but at the same time it felt like there was another voice speaking through me. How can that be?"

As we said, the Force of Self-Expression comes through your Shadow. But there's something wonderful about this higher force: *It speaks through you in a way that is unique to you*. It gives each of us a distinctive voice—and yet all our voices derive from the same ultimate source. That's why true self-expression feels like it's coming from someplace else—and simultaneously makes you more yourself.

For her entire life, Jennifer had experienced speaking out as uncomfortable—it threatened to expose what she was most ashamed of, her Shadow. Now things were reversed: speaking out was an opportunity to become fully herself. As she put it, "I guess I can't even *find* my real self unless I express it."

Exactly.

In fact, the ancients saw self-expression as the fundamental quality of the universe. In Genesis, God is portrayed as a self-expressive being. God *says* let there be light, and light is created. God *says* let the earth bring forth plants and trees, and it does.

So it's when you're expressing yourself that you're most in harmony with the universe. You feel you belong to it. For Jennifer, this meant she stopped questioning her value as a human being; she was no longer an inferior outsider with nothing to say.

She also began to experience herself as part of a community. She found that people respected her and sought her advice. It was the Shadow that enabled her to have this newfound impact on others.

The Shadow makes true human connection possible—it's the part of us we all share. Without it, we exaggerate our differences from others; we feel separate from them. Relationships—between different individuals, religions, nations—can work only when we use our Shadows to create a universal bond. Doing this puts us in a state where even opponents can acknowledge the humanity in each other. It's the only way we can enjoy the freedom to be different and still coexist with one another.

This fellowship is possible because the Shadow speaks a language that is common to all of humanity—a language of the heart rather than one of words. Because you have a Shadow, you already know this language. Two friends of yours can speak the same exact words of support, but you know the difference when one truly empathizes with you and the other is disengaged or impatient. One friend has her heart in it while the other doesn't.

This language of the heart is alluded to in the biblical story of the Tower of Babel. The story depicts an earlier race of people who spoke "a single language" and lived a unified existence.

It was a gift—this state of unity; but these ancient people misused it, proposing to build a monument to their power: a tower that would reach right up into heaven. Foiling their ambition, God "confuse[d] their language [so] that they [could no longer] understand one another's speech . . . and scattered them over the face of the earth." The common interpretation of this story is that it depicts the origin of different languages. But there's a deeper meaning in it: *Even those who spoke the same language could no longer understand each other; they had lost the shared language of the heart.*

We, who are alive now, are the end product of this alienation, and our lives are much the worse for it. We've lost the universal language of the heart, and with it, any sense of an all-inclusive human community. We've lost the sense that we're on the same team and that we have a duty to something higher than ourselves. Public officials no longer feel bound to place the public interest over their own; divorce attorneys inflame conflict to get higher fees; doctors order unnecessary tests to protect themselves. Our public discourse has degenerated into a no-holds-barred attack zone, where nothing is off-limits—whether it's an opponent's patriotism, appearance, or private life.

But we have an opportunity to heal this. The communal language with which we can reach one another still lives in the Shadow. This idea was thrilling to Jennifer. For the first time in her life, she was able to feel what it was like to have an impact on other people. As a society, we tend to associate influence with important people in positions of power. As Jennifer put it, "I thought you had to be famous to have an impact." This assumption is understandable—but it's a costly mistake. It means we ignore the ordinary, prosaic opportunities to encourage, connect with, and inspire one another. You can use Inner Authority to become a positive force for the people around you—whether it's inspiring self-discipline in your children, connecting with an elder who's lonely, or even bringing some lightness to an encounter with a stranger.

Another misunderstanding is that you can only have a real impact on someone by dominating them. Empathizing with how they feel tends to be seen as a sign of weakness. As Jennifer joked grimly, "My father had only one way of wielding his authority—he used a belt." That kind of leadership breeds a fear and resentment that eventually weakens it.

There's a way to be a strong leader without engendering fear and resentment. If your authority is based on the Shadow, you can stay in touch with how others feel. When people feel understood, they want to do what you ask of them even if they don't fully agree. Empathy now enhances your authority. This is true regardless of the context—whether it's with your friends, family, community, etc. In fact, even big business recognizes the value of honoring others' points of view—it builds real, lasting teamwork.

The community Jennifer was beginning to experience is called the "Social Matrix." It's an interconnected web of human beings that generates healing energy that can't be created any other way. The more connected we feel to each other, the happier we are. There's even research indicating that people who feel a sense of community live longer and enjoy greater physical and mental health.

But there's a deeper benefit as well.

Hidden inside the dynamics of the Social Matrix is the solution to the fundamental problem facing the human race: how do we remain unified without sacrificing our individual freedom? The answer lies with the Shadow. It carries the unique individuality of our inner self, yet it lives in a space of complete connection with everyone else's Shadow. But unless we each take personal responsibility for activating our Shadow, these remain only potentials. If we fail to make the right choice, we face a slow descent into the primal, violent hell the philosopher Thomas Hobbes aptly called, "the war of all against all."

FREQUENTLY ASKED QUESTIONS

1. I can sense my Shadow's presence, but I can't see it.

This isn't unusual. Some people are less visual than others. If you can't see your Shadow, just practice feeling its presence right in front of you.

Then, when you use Inner Authority, direct your attention to wherever that presence is. Over time, what starts as a presence will take on a visual form.

Some people have the opposite problem. They can see an image of their Shadow, but it doesn't seem to have any real presence; it can look like a stick figure or cartoon character.

In our experience, this problem can always be solved through repetition. Treat the image as if it's real, even if it doesn't feel real, and eventually it will.

2. I can see my Shadow when my eyes are closed, but not when they're open and I'm in front of people.

This is also a common problem. It takes some getting used to—seeing the audience with your physical eyes while you see the Shadow in your imagination. But the truth is, everyone knows how to do this. Every time you get absorbed in a good work of fiction, your physical eyes are scanning the words on the page, but in your imagination you can see the characters and their surroundings vividly.

You will develop the same ability when you use Inner Authority. As you practice it repeatedly, seeing your Shadow with your eyes open will become second nature.

3. Won't concentrating on my Shadow separate me from the audience and put me in my own world?

Actually, it's the opposite. Feeling intensely connected to your Shadow gives you an inner sense of confidence that dissolves your fear of the audience. This frees you to connect to them. It's when you try to hide your Shadow that you become terrified of the audience. That's what puts you in your own world.

In the practice of psychotherapy, both Phil and I regularly see our Shadows, right in the middle of a session with a patient. And we have never been accused of seeming distracted, unfocused, or in another world.

4. Is this practice going to turn me into a split personality?

The term *split personality* has a specific connotation for mental-health professionals. For them, it connotes severe psychological problems that are beyond the scope of this book.

But when a layperson asks if Inner Authority is going to turn him into a "split personality," he means something different. He's afraid there's something wrong with having a second self inside him, and he feels uncomfortable talking to it. He's afraid doing that makes him crazy.

But the truth is the opposite. Everyone has a Shadow. What's really crazy is to deny the existence of it. You're ignoring your entire inner self. When you embrace the Shadow, it's actually a tremendous relief. Even better, you're on the road to developing powers you've never had before.

When you start this process, don't be dissuaded by the fear that there's anything wrong with you. If you can keep it up even for a few weeks, you'll feel the opposite—that *you're going sane.*

5. **Won't connecting to my Shadow have a bad effect on me?** There was a time in my life when I *became* like my Shadow, and it wasn't good. I just gave in to my worst tendencies.

This is an almost universal objection to Inner Authority. The Shadow is repugnant to us. And the fear is that the more we interact with it the more we're going to become like it.

The fear is understandable; most people can remember a troubled time in their life when the Shadow overwhelmed them. Generally, these are periods when you withdraw from the world; you become listless, you feel inferior or purposeless, as though you've lost your way. You might also overindulge in food or alcohol. Anything can trigger this state—a rejection, a setback. But often it simply comes over you without explanation. The first time people experience it is frequently in adolescence but it can happen anytime.

At times like these, you become your Shadow—it has hijacked your life.

When that happens, most people don't know that there's an alternative. Phil felt that Jung was aware of the positive potential in the Shadow but had never developed a practical and reliable method to bring it out. Achieving that required a way to work with your Shadow—rather than becoming it. That's where Inner Authority comes in; it makes your Shadow your partner. *When the Shadow becomes your partner, its nature changes.* Only then does it become the source of free, spontaneous self-expression. Without this tool, the Shadow is nothing more than the sum total of your worst tendencies.

If you use Inner Authority consistently, you create an ongoing *relationship* with the Shadow. Think of it as a partnership where each party is supplying something the other can't. The Shadow brings the ability to express itself with passion—something you can't do on your own. But you bring to the Shadow something it needs but can't supply for itself: acknowledgment of its powers. You give this to the Shadow every time you choose to use the tool.

When you put these energies together, you end up with a whole that's more than the sum of its parts. As strange as it might seem, the "best you," the highest version of yourself, is only present when you're in this ongoing partnership with your Shadow. This is the real meaning of the term *Higher Self.* Its secret is that the Higher Self is the combination of two opposites, you and your Shadow.

If this partnership falls apart—or is never formed—you end up in an unbalanced state. On one hand, the Shadow takes over and overwhelms you with its tendencies toward inferiority, weakness, and depression. For obvious reasons, Phil called this a "takeover." On the other hand, you banish the Shadow completely and live a superficial life, craving the approval of others and unable to express yourself deeply. It's common to swing from one of these extremes to the other without ever putting the two pieces together. Tragically, most people think these are their only two choices.

But creating a balanced relationship with the Shadow isn't one choice or the other, it's a process. You need to work on your partnership with the Shadow all the time. Inner Authority is the key to doing this.

6. How do I work with my Shadow if it looks enraged, destructive, or hateful?

Remember, the Shadow is an image of everything you don't want to be. In this chapter, we're dealing with its most common manifestation, which we call the "inferior Shadow." Inferiority and insecurity are the most common feelings we have when we're trying to express ourselves in front of other people.

But there's another thing we don't want to be. We don't want to see ourselves as "bad" or "evil." By "evil," we mean the part of you that has an impulse to act out of pure self-interest without regard to anyone or anything that gets in the way. This manifests itself in selfishness, greed, or, when your aims are thwarted, hatred or destructive rage. These qualities comprise a second Shadow, which we call the "evil Shadow." The fact that you have an evil Shadow doesn't mean you're evil any more than having an inferior Shadow means you're inferior. But it's a part of every person. The key is that it's socially unacceptable, and therefore we don't like to admit it's there.

In a future book we'll teach you how to prevent the evil Shadow from acting destructively. But in the meantime, if that's the dominant form that your Shadow takes, you can definitely use it in the same way we've described for the inferior Shadow. Not only will this work, but for many people it will be the first time they've been able to use the evil Shadow constructively.

7. I've read Jung and it was eye-opening for me. But your application of the Shadow concept is so different from classical Jungian therapy. Why is that?

I want to make it clear that Jung's work represented a monumental breakthrough. Not only did he expand the notion of what's in the human unconscious, he developed a bold, new way to work with it. When images from the unconscious emerged, rather than intellectually analyzing them, Jung would encourage the patient to interact with them. He called this "Active Imagination." His goal was to integrate these figures—including the Shadow—into the patient's sense of himself, making him whole. He called this state the "Self."

It was a very fruitful approach that went far beyond the psychotherapy that was practiced at the time. My only problem with it was that it could be undirected at times. This was especially apparent when it came to integrating the Shadow. Patients needed clear instructions for accessing its immense power and bringing it to their lives as they were lived daily. It was too important to leave to chance. Phil had taken the next step and developed a reliable way to make that connection through a set of tools that could bring the Shadow's power to bear when it was most needed.

The tools take advantage of the fact that the Shadow is a separate being, with its own sensitivity and worldview. It needs and deserves the same attention you'd bring to a relationship with another human being. By using Active Imagination, Jung took the brilliant first step toward nurturing that relationship. But there was still a problem. The events of our lives distract us from the inner world, cutting off our relationship with the Shadow. Phil felt it was possible to use the same events to deepen the relationship with the Shadow. Freezing in front of an audience is one such event. Inner Authority makes the Shadow the solution to the problem and in so doing, strengthens your relationship with it. The most profound way to acknowledge the Shadow is to make it part of your moment-to-moment life.

OTHER USES OF INNER AUTHORITY

Inner Authority lets you overcome initial shyness, particularly around people you're interested in romantically. *Many people who have a lot to offer in a relationship never give themselves the chance to get into one—the act of meeting someone new is too frightening. The people who get the most opportunities to connect romantically aren't those who make the best partners; they're those who put themselves out there the most.*

Jim suffered from a lifetime of crippling shyness. Meeting new people was unpleasant; social events were frightening. But he was most handicapped when it came to the opposite sex. Seeing that he was tall, handsome, and obviously sensitive, women often gave him a chance to approach them, but he would freeze every time. Paralyzed with self-consciousness, he could manage only a sickly half smile. They would misinterpret this as condescension or lack of interest and put up their own defenses. This just made him more self-conscious. When he began work on his Shadow, it appeared to him as a grotesque monster, but seeing it clearly was a relief for him. He started to practice Inner Authority alone—it was a big step for him to even try it in front of a mirror. When he did, to his surprise, he felt that for the first time he could look himself in the eye. From there, he began to practice on shopkeepers and passersby, since the stakes were low. Months later, he got to the point where he could talk to women without freezing—soon he had a social life.

Inner Authority lets you express need and vulnerability. *Many people, especially males, hide behind a facade that says they have life under control and need nothing from others. Life* *has a way of breaking down this facade and putting you in a position where you must ask for help. Those who can't ask for help risk losing everything.*

Harold was a successful real-estate developer with a huge ego. He took on large projects that put him at financial risk. When the economy was good, this approach worked well. He lived a lavish and flamboyant lifestyle, only feeling secure when he was the center of attention, pontificating to others. Then real estate went bad and the banks called in his loans. Without money, he found he had few friends. To avoid bankruptcy, he had to turn to his father, who was in the same business but was modest and conservative—and as a result had substantial savings. Harold prided himself on having surpassed his father; asking him for money would shatter his big-shot facade. Inner Authority, which allowed him to communicate from his real inner self, taught him he could function without the facade. After a lot of practice, he was able to ask his father for help. "It was the first honest moment I've had since I was a kid," Harold said. His action won the respect of his father. By using Inner Authority every time he talked to him, Harold was able to have a real relationship with his father from then on.

Inner Authority allows you to connect to your loved ones with more emotion. *The way you communicate, especially the emotion you express, is more important than the words you use. When you speak without emotion, you can't have enough impact on others to form a real connection.*

Joe was an accomplished radiologist. Other doctors sought him out to diagnose their patients. Meticulously careful, he picked up things others overlooked. But he was more at home with computer images than he was with human beings. This was acceptable for a radiologist but not for a parent. When Joe's oldest child was thirteen, she became unwilling to spend time with him. He was hurt, but when he asked her what was wrong she stormed out of the room. She told her mother that her father didn't like her—and that he was a nerd; he'd stared blankly when she'd worn a grown-up dress for the first time. He tried to make up for this by mechanically telling her that he loved her, but she was unmoved. His wife told him it wasn't his words that were lacking but his feelings. Feelings were a mystery to him until he met his Shadow. It held all the emotions he was out of touch with. He began to use Inner Authority every time he spoke to his daughter. He was astounded at the effect this had on their relationship. As they grew closer, she developed the confidence that came from knowing her father loved her.

Inner Authority activates a higher force in the act of writing, not just speaking. *Writer's block happens when writers become more interested in the outcome of their efforts than in the process of writing. It usually takes the form of a frustrated attempt to make their work perfect and harsh self-criticism when they fail.*

Julie loved writing screenplays and wondered if she could make it a career. To her surprise, the first one she submitted was bought and made into an acclaimed movie. She was then offered a large amount of money to write a script for a famous director. She now felt pressure to come up with something as good as her first one. Writing was no longer fun. Instead of trusting her instincts, she got caught in her head, trying to figure out what would please others. She became highly critical of anything she wrote. Her attacks on her own work became so vicious, she no longer wanted to write at all. The only solution was to reconnect to the part of her that loved to write for its own sake—her Shadow. She did this by using Inner Authority throughout her writing sessions. She directed the tool at whomever she imagined would be reading the script. She was especially careful to use the tool the moment she began to attack herself. Inner Authority was bringing a higher force—the Force of Self-Expression—into her writing. She stopped fearing what others would think about her work; writing became fun again.

SUMMARY OF INNER AUTHORITY

What the Tool Is For
In intimidating situations, when you find it difficult to express yourself or even connect with other people. These are moments when you "freeze," become wooden or stiff, unable to express yourself in a natural, spontaneous way. Underlying this is an irrational sense of insecurity. The tool allows you to overcome the insecurity and be yourself.

What You're Fighting Against
Insecurity is a universal but badly misunderstood human trait. We think we know what's making us insecure—our appearance, level of education, or socio-economic status. In fact, there's something deep inside us that is the cause of all insecurity. It's called the Shadow—the embodiment of all our negative traits—and we're terrified that someone will see it. As a consequence, we expend a lot of energy hiding it, which makes it impossible for us to be ourselves. The tool gives us a new way to deal with the problem of having a Shadow.

Cues to Use the Tool
1. Whenever you feel performance anxiety. This could be triggered by social events, confrontations, speaking in public.
2. Use the tool right before the event as well as during it.

3. A less-obvious cue would be when you're anticipating the event and worrying about it.

The Tool in Brief

1. Standing in front of any kind of audience, see your Shadow off to one side, facing you. (It works just as well with an imaginary audience or an audience composed of only one person.) Ignore the audience completely and focus all of your attention on the Shadow. Feel an unbreakable bond between the two of you—as a unit you're fearless.
2. Together, you and the Shadow forcefully turn toward the audience and silently command them to "LISTEN!" Feel the authority that comes when you and your Shadow speak with one voice.

The Higher Force You're Using

The Force of Self-Expression allows us to reveal ourselves in a truthful, genuine way—without caring about others' approval. It speaks through us with unusual clarity and authority, but it also expresses itself nonverbally, like when an athlete is "in the zone." In adults, this force gets buried in the Shadow. The tool, by connecting you to the Shadow, enables you to resurrect the force and have it flow through you.

CHAPTER 5

The Tool:
The Grateful Flow

The Higher Force:
Gratefulness

ELIZABETH, A NEW PATIENT OF MINE, HAD BEEN up all night worrying. "I'm having the whole family over for Thanksgiving tomorrow, and I'm pretty sure the turkey will be ruined," she said as she wrung her hands so hard I thought her skin would come off.

"You already started cooking it?" I asked.

"No, but the last time I prepared the turkey, my cousin got food poisoning."

She looked at me beseechingly for a moment, but before I could say a word, her mind, churning with anxieties, was on to other pressing matters. A distant cousin announced, at the last moment, that he was bringing a guest—this would supposedly double her workload. Her gluten-intolerant nephew wouldn't be able to eat any stuffing. How was she going to seat her left-wing father away from her right-wing brother as well as from her emotionally fragile cousin whom her dad always managed to offend?

On and on, her worries spilled out like staccato gunfire, as if she were in a race with Armageddon. For a second, I lost focus on what she was saying and caught a glimpse of her inner world—a hellish place where incessant dark thoughts bound her in a web of doom. It made me sad for her. "I see how much stress you're feeling," I ventured reassuringly, "but I doubt it's as dire as you think."

"You sound like my husband," she fired back. "It's easy for him to say—all he has to do is pour drinks and make sure the TV's on in time for the kickoff."

I felt useless for most of the session, but surprisingly, Elizabeth thanked me at the end and promised to return next week. I started the next session by asking how Thanksgiving had gone, but she waved her hand dismissively, now preoccupied with a new crisis, a rash on her leg that she was sure indicated lupus.

Elizabeth was always worried about something. Whatever it was—the strange noise her car made when she started it, the headaches that surely were caused by a brain tumor—worry was the focal point of her existence.

There had been a time in her life when she'd been relatively free of worry—when she was in school. Elizabeth had always excelled in academics, earning a Masters in Psychology with almost perfect grades. But by the time she graduated, she was married with a child, and she had to enter the working world and help support her family.

After a long search, she found a job as a guidance counselor at a community college. The salary was low, but she was perfectly suited for the job—academically adept and very concerned about the students under her care. Maybe too concerned.

With a huge caseload, there was no way to give each student the attention she felt they needed. But she did find the time to worry about them. Was this one taking the right courses? Was that one in a depression she'd failed to pick up? Should she work Saturdays to catch up? But how would she find time for her own daughter? Despite this dire picture, she was a beloved counselor and had escaped another fear—getting fired—for fourteen years and running.

I asked what living with her fears was like for her husband. "Sometimes he laughs, but usually his eyes just glaze over," she admitted. Recently, however, he wasn't taking it as well. There was a meeting at their daughter's school that neither parent could make because of work schedules. Over dinner, Elizabeth couldn't stop talking about it, bringing herself to the edge of panic. He suddenly burst out angrily, "These are ordinary problems, and you're acting like our whole life is unraveling!"

"What do you think about what he said?" I asked.

Her eyes welled up with tears. "I know he's right. My

worrying must be hard on everyone around me. But just imagine what it's like for *me*."

THE BLACK CLOUD

Elizabeth had the haunted look of someone whose life was falling apart. Actually, it was quite stable—and in the crucial areas it was blessed. Her husband was a decorated police officer with enough time in to make it impossible for him to lose his job. Completely devoted to her and their daughter, he lived to make sure they were safe and comfortable. Neither he nor Elizabeth cared about life's luxuries—in a material sense they had everything they needed. But it made no difference how attentive he was, she experienced life as a series of calamities that she faced alone.

Her fears (no matter how far-fetched) felt real to her because she lived in a world of her own making. To an extent, we all do this. We like to think we react to the world as it is, when really we react to a world that exists in our own minds. This inner world is so powerful, it overwhelms our ability to see reality. John Milton, in *Paradise Lost*, expressed it this way: "The mind is its own place, and in itself / Can make a Heav'n of Hell, a Hell of Heav'n."

I wanted to demonstrate to Elizabeth how this inner world worked. I asked her to close her eyes and replay her most recent worry. "I heard a radio report about the polar ice caps melting. . . . I'm thinking we should move inland, to higher ground." I asked her to put aside that specific worry and see if she felt anything *behind* the worries.

Startled, she opened her eyes. "I felt this heavy darkness around me, like a cloud of doom." I told her to try the same thing with a different worry—whether her daughter was going to get her college applications in on time. She tried it and to her surprise, she felt the exact same darkness around her.

We call this presence the "Black Cloud." When you worry incessantly, regardless of the subject, you're creating a negative energy that hangs over you like a cloud. The Black Cloud screens out everything positive and creates a sense of impending doom. It makes no difference if the doom comes through natural disaster, disease, or human error.

Elizabeth was an extreme example of how dominating the Black Cloud can become. Its power doesn't come from the truth of its predictions—they're almost always false. The Black Cloud dominates us in a much more primal way—through the force of repetition. If you repeat something enough times, it becomes a habit with a life of its own—it's easier to do it than not.

You can have your own experience of the Black Cloud. Start by picking something you typically worry about. Maybe it's your job, a troubled child, or a parent who's unwell.

> Close your eyes and re-create the worried
> thoughts, repeating them intensely like you do in
> real life. At first, this might feel artificial, but if you
> keep at it, the thoughts will gain momentum and
> acquire a life of their own. Now, focus on the inner
> state that these thoughts have created. What does
> it feel like?

You just experienced a mild version of the Black Cloud. When it occurs in your actual life, it's darker and more oppressive. By blotting out everything positive, it convinces you that only the negative is real. The following illustration depicts the Black Cloud at work:

Above the cloud is the sun, the universal symbol for the positive. Here, it would represent all that is right in the world. We've drawn the Black Cloud as an impenetrable shroud that keeps out the positive. The sun is still shining, but for the person under the cloud, it doesn't exist. There is no joy; only negativity. He's bent over by the heaviness of the dark world his thoughts have created. There's a huge price to pay for living this way.

For the person crushed by the Black Cloud, there can be no peace of mind.

THE PRICE OF NEGATIVITY

For most of us, peace of mind is a precious feeling. It is the sense that everything is in its right place, that "all is well." You've felt this in fleeting moments—everyone has—an inner serenity, a sense that you're in harmony with all of existence.

The Black Cloud annihilates this sense of peace. Under its spell, all you can see is what's not right with the world. Any kind of negative thinking can do this—hopelessness, self-hatred, judgmentalism—but worry does it best.

Without a sense of serenity, everything becomes a crisis. With all your energy focused on survival, enjoying life is a luxury you can't afford. Elizabeth couldn't settle in with a good book, take in a movie, or meet a friend for lunch—there was always a dire problem demanding her attention. One day she looked up at me, exhausted, and admitted the truth: "I can't remember the last time anything gave me real joy."

There's a cruel twist to this pattern of perpetual crisis. In the Black Cloud, every problem is of life-and-death importance—but no one can see this but you. You can't trust anyone to help with your problems because no one takes them as seriously as you do. Inevitably, you're left feeling overwhelmed and alone.

Elizabeth reached the point where she couldn't rely on her own husband. She came to her session exhausted. "I'm dead on my feet," she complained. "I don't know how I'm going to do the laundry today."

I was confused. "I thought your husband filled in when you needed help around the house."

"I've stopped asking him to help. He doesn't fold the clothes right. It's easier to do it myself."

This attitude just made her husband—already frustrated by her exaggerated fears—more alienated. No one likes feeling useless. Her friends were dropping away, too—she had no time for them.

Fortunately, right after Elizabeth started therapy, something happened that gave her the shock she needed—it concerned her daughter. Elizabeth had edited her college essays, kept her apprised of application deadlines, even helped her stamp and address envelopes. So Elizabeth was shocked when her daughter accused her of being a "selfish nag." When they had both calmed down, her daughter explained. "I'm sorry I called you that. But you've got to understand. Most of the time it feels like you aren't doing it for me—

you're doing it to deal with *your own anxiety* about me getting into college."

This was a turning point for Elizabeth. She could no longer deny that the Black Cloud had twisted her strongest impulse as a parent into something that was burdensome to her daughter. If it could spoil her parenting, it could spoil anything. She became determined to free herself from the Black Cloud.

But this was harder than she expected.

WHY IS NEGATIVE THINKING SO POWERFUL?

It's tempting to think we can change our thought patterns easily. After all, why can't we just replace each negative thought with a positive one? This idea has always been part of American culture, reaching its peak with a book called *The Power of Positive Thinking*. Unfortunately, it's one of those ideas that seems like it would work but doesn't. It fails because, *in real life, positive thoughts don't have anywhere near the power that negative thoughts do.*

Elizabeth discovered this on her own when a friend gave her a book on the subject. "For three days I tried to think positive thoughts." She frowned. "But every time I tried, I felt stupid for pretending everything was okay when there were dangers everywhere. I don't know why they call it the power of positive thinking—the negative thoughts have all the power."

What is this power? To find out, I asked her to close her eyes and create a succession of worries. She nodded. "Now let your mind relax, as if you've lost the ability to worry. What does that feel like?"

Elizabeth flinched. "I felt myself relaxing for a second, then . . . it felt like I lost control of everything."

"Okay. Now—right in the midst of that out-of-control feeling—reintroduce the worrying. How does that feel?"

"Actually . . . a little better." She opened her eyes. "When I'm worrying, somehow it feels like I can fend off the bad things. It reminds me of when I was a little girl and I would stay up all night imagining how terrible it would be if my parents split up. It became a ritual. I really believed that, as long as I worried about it, it wouldn't happen."

"But your parents split up. Your worrying failed, but you kept at it."

"I guess I was afraid that, if I stopped, then bad things were *sure* to happen."

In essence, worry had become a powerful superstition—with no more real benefit than a rabbit's foot. But superstitions have a powerful appeal because they give us a magical sense that we can affect the future. Of course, this is an illusion—most of life is beyond our ability to predict, much less control. From a picnic getting rained out to a sudden heart attack—anything can happen at any time. Still, we insist we can control the uncontrollable.

Why?

Because of a basic assumption about the universe that we

never question. We assume (because science tells us so) that the universe is indifferent to us. Based only on what we see around us, this is a reasonable conclusion. But it makes us feel alone in a universe that doesn't care about us. Feeling we won't be provided for, we become obsessed with controlling our future. In that context, worrying seems to make sense.

But what if, on a level we can't see, the universe *is* interested in our welfare, supporting us in ways large and small? It's not that much of a stretch to be able to perceive this. Start with your physical body. It extracts oxygen from the air, it digests complex foods, it allows you the miracle of sight and hearing. All these things work amazingly well without your even understanding how. There's more—the earth supplies us with food, the air we breathe; and it gives us the raw materials with which to build things. And these are just a few examples of the infinite number of ways our existence is sustained by the universe.

When I told this to Elizabeth, she said, "Other people have told me this, but I just can't feel it."

Elizabeth wasn't alone in this. A true feeling for the beneficence of the universe doesn't come naturally to most people. Fortunately, there is a way that anyone can experience the endless generosity of the universe.

THE HIGHER FORCE: GRATEFULNESS

Very early in life, something happened to Phil which led him to experience the universe in this new way. Eventually, it led to his being able to guide others to the same experience. Here it is in his own words:

_____

As I explained in Chapter 1, when I was nine years old, my brother died of a rare type of cancer. After that, my family waited helplessly for another catastrophe to befall us. Who was next? Then, when I was fourteen, unexplained headaches began to strike just as I fell asleep each night. They felt like a knife sticking through my skull. My first thought was that I had a brain tumor. As the weeks passed, my terror grew, but to protect my parents, I kept it to myself. It finally became too much, and I told them. Terrified, they put me through a complete medical workup.

When all the tests came back negative, I knew I was fine. What I didn't know was that my experience of life was about to be permanently changed.

Until this ordeal, the most meaningful thing in my life was basketball. The best games were at the YMCA, but to get there, I had to take a bus through a decaying part of Manhattan. Every corner was staked out by streetwalkers and dope dealers. Like every native New Yorker, I dealt with the danger by staring straight ahead and shutting out whatever was happening around me. A few blocks before my destination, I reached an area where every building had been reduced to rubble—the beginning of a large construction project. It was actually a relief.

I remember getting on that bus the first night after my life had been spared. It lurched forward on its usual course through hell, the same shouts and sirens echoing on the streets outside; the air still stinking of garbage. But because I thought I'd never take this ride again, I experienced it in a whole new light. Every sensation felt like a miracle. Something had given me back this ride—and with it the rest of my life. My heart was overcome with gratitude.

Phil's experience was so strong, it forced him to look at everything differently. One moment he was getting on a dirty bus. A moment later, everything was given back to him. He was in the presence of an all-giving power.

We call this power "the Source." Phil experienced it in one brief flash, but it's always there. It created everything you can see. Most miraculously, it created life and it remains intimately involved with all the living beings it created. This includes you. In the past it gave you life; in the present it sustains you; and its creative power fills your future with infinite possibilities.

Once you can recognize all that you're given, you feel connected to the Source. Then, you aren't so alone and your need to worry diminishes.

When I explained all of this to Elizabeth, she seemed

dubious. "I've always envied people who could believe in what you're talking about—it seems really comforting. But I'm too much of a skeptic. I mean, how can you be sure this 'Source' exists?"

That was a good question. Normally, for us to believe something exists, we have to see it with our own eyes (or perceive it with one of our other physical senses).

The problem is the Source isn't in the physical world. It exists in a spiritual world, which our five physical senses can't perceive. To experience the Source, we need a new kind of perception, and Phil's story reveals the nature of it. At the sudden realization that his life had been given back to him, his heart was overwhelmed with gratitude. It was this sense of gratefulness—not anything he saw or heard—that gave him a personal connection with the all-giving Source.

On one level, gratefulness was his *reaction* to the generosity of the Source. But on a more profound level, gratefulness was the means by which he *perceived* the Source. At first, it might seem strange to think of gratefulness as a means of perception, rather than just an emotional reaction. But with practice, you'll find that gratefulness perceives the spiritual world just as clearly as your eyes and ears perceive the physical world.

This makes gratefulness much more important than a mere emotion; it makes gratefulness a higher force. In general, higher forces allow you to *do* things you never thought you could do. In this case, gratefulness allows you to *perceive* things you never thought you could perceive. In short, gratefulness is a higher organ of perception, through which you can accurately appreciate a fundamental truth: *the universe works—mysteriously—and you're the constant beneficiary of its generosity.* The Source is supporting you every moment from the day you're born until the day you die. To feel grateful for that relationship isn't about good manners, it's a whole new way of perceiving reality.

THE TOOL: THE GRATEFUL FLOW

There are times in everyone's life when the Source makes its presence known so powerfully that we feel grateful without any effort on our part. For you, it might have happened while camping out under a starry sky; or maybe when your child was born. What makes these moments truly special is the deep feeling that something was being given to you; something you couldn't have created yourself. Think back to some time this happened in your life, and re-create the experience right now, with your eyes closed.

> Visualize everything that was happening around you. Focus on the gratefulness you were feeling at the time. Now, connect that gratefulness to the presence of an unimaginably generous force.

Many of us have experienced the Source this way. But no matter how powerfully we felt it, it happened under special circumstances that can rarely be re-created. If you're serious about defeating your negativity, you need access to the Source at all times, no matter what the circumstances. The only way to gain that access is to learn to activate your sense of gratefulness at will.

Here's the tool to awaken the organ of gratefulness.

The Grateful Flow

Pick out things in your life you can be grateful for—particularly things you'd normally take for granted. Say them to yourself silently, slowly enough to feel the value of each one. "I'm grateful for my eyesight; I'm grateful I have hot water," etc. You should do this until you've mentioned at least five items—it takes less than thirty seconds. Feel the slight strain of your effort to find these items.

You should feel the gratefulness you express flowing upward, directly from your heart. Then, when you've finished mentioning the specific items, your heart should continue to generate gratefulness, this time without words. The energy you are now giving out is the Grateful Flow.

As this energy emanates from your heart, your chest will soften and open. In this state you'll feel yourself approaching an overwhelming presence, filled with the power of infinite giving. You've made a connection to the Source.

The picture below shows how the tool works. It creates a sense of gratefulness that's so powerful it penetrates the Black Cloud. This is illustrated by the channel that extends upward from the person, splitting the Cloud. The small lines inside the channel represent the force of gratefulness, flowing upward. In the earlier drawing (p. 146), the sun shining above the Cloud represented whatever was right with the world. Now we can give the sun its proper name: the Source, the creator of all that is, the ultimate positive force in the universe. This picture shows how gratefulness becomes an organ that connects us to the Source.

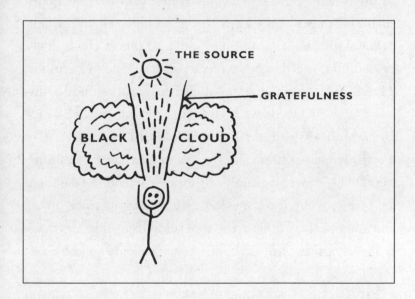

We call the tool the "Grateful Flow." *Flow* refers to any process that's endlessly creative. In the tool, you create an endless flow of thoughts to stimulate an endless flow of gratefulness, which affirms the ceaseless generosity of the Source. Since flow is always creating, it has a quality of constant renewal. That's why it's important to name different items you're grateful for each time you use the tool. Coming up with at least a few new items each time requires effort, but it's a sacred effort that keeps you deeply connected to the Source.

At first it might seem difficult to come up with things you're grateful for, but it's easier than you think. You can use things that aren't happening, such as "I'm grateful I'm not in a war zone" or "I'm grateful I don't live on the San Andreas fault." And you can also mine your past for items, such as "I'm grateful I went to a good high school" or "I'm grateful my mother loved me." Stick to things you're truly grateful for, not things you feel you *should* be grateful for. These are often minor things that you might not notice unless they were taken away—like the fact that you had a nice lunch with a friend, for example, or that your electricity works. Patients often ask why we emphasize these minor items. The answer is simple: although we tend to take them for granted, *they're always there.* By forcing us to be aware and appreciative of them, the tool reminds us that *the Source is always there as well—sustaining us in an unimaginable number of ways.*

When you're learning the tool, start by mechanically naming things you're grateful for. Once you get used to that, try to feel gratefulness emanating from your heart as you name the specific things. Once you can feel that, then you can stop the words for a moment and train your heart to generate pure gratefulness without words. It's that final state that will open you up to the presence of the Source. After some practice you'll move seamlessly through the tool. Then you can start using it in daily life.

When you go about your day, pay attention to your thoughts. At the first sign of negative thinking, use the Grateful Flow; negativity is your cue. Remember, the purpose of a cue is to get you to use the tool immediately, even if it doesn't seem urgent. This is particularly important with the Grateful Flow because negative thinking puts most of us into the Black Cloud without our even being aware of it. Elizabeth's worries, for example, would often start with an innocent-seeming observation: "That's a mole on my arm." Then it would escalate: "I'm pretty sure it's new—and it looks dark and irregular." In no time her mind was out of control: "It's a melanoma, it's spreading. . . . Oh, my God, I'm going to die!" Once she trained herself to use the Grateful Flow immediately, after the first or second thought, she gained much more control over her mind. For most people, this is the first experience they've had with being able to defeat their negative thoughts.

Elizabeth's negativity mostly consisted of worry, but it's good to get into the habit of using the tool to interrupt *all* negative thinking. This could include self-criticism ("I'm so stupid"), judgment ("That girl is so ugly"), or complaining ("I'm so tired of my job"). Obsessing, no matter what it's about, is another form of negative thinking that can be arrested with the Grateful Flow.

The Grateful Flow is so important, you should also make it a daily practice. One way to do this is to use the tool at specific times throughout the day. Many patients use it first thing when they wake up, with each meal, and last thing before they fall asleep.

You can also use it whenever your mind is undirected, which can happen throughout the day—while riding the bus, taking a coffee break, or standing in line at a convenience store. Once you use the Grateful Flow at these times, you'll see how undisciplined the mind is. Left to its own devices, it degenerates, filling itself with trivia, insecurity, and negativity.

The point of using the Grateful Flow so frequently is to make you the master of your own mind, the only thing a human being can really control. *Until you can control your mind, you're spiritually immature.* As children, we need parents to make us brush our teeth and wash ourselves every day. As adults, we accept our responsibility for these things without question. With practice, you'll bring the same diligence to your spiritual hygiene as you do to your physical hygiene. At that point you'll become a spiritual adult.

When gratefulness becomes a way of life, the Source becomes a constant companion. The ancients expressed this companionship in very personal terms. In Psalm 23 King David wrote: "Yea, though I walk through the valley of the shadow of death, / I will fear no evil, / for Thou art with me; Thy rod and Thy staff, they comfort me." Living in modern times, you might not experience the Source in such an intimate, personal way, but you will feel the kind of comfort, support, and nurturing that King David expressed so eloquently.

Connecting to the Source is a bit different than connecting to the higher forces we discussed in Chapters 2–4. This is because the Source is the highest thing in the universe and in fact, created those forces. We can't imitate the Source as we can those forces because ultimately, it's unknowable. The best we can do is put ourselves in a grateful state, acknowledging the gifts it has given us; *gifts we couldn't possibly have created ourselves*. So for this tool only, the feeling of gratefulness itself is the connecting rod that allows you to sense the Source's presence.

THE SECRET BENEFITS OF CONNECTING TO THE SOURCE

Elizabeth practiced the Grateful Flow assiduously. She was making progress but still spent too much time in the Black Cloud. Then one day she arrived for a session fifteen minutes late. Normally she would've been beating herself up and talking even faster than normal to cram everything in. But she seemed relaxed, even pleased. "I just had lunch with an old friend of mine, someone I haven't seen in years. We got to talking, and suddenly I looked at my watch and couldn't believe it—two hours had passed . . . two hours without worry or stress. I realized I was happy for the first time since I could remember." She was glowing. "Then I started worrying about being late to therapy, and I used the Grateful Flow again. This powerful calm came over me. My mind was perfectly clear."

Once Elizabeth learned how to create that sense of calm, she was able to reproduce it when she needed it. From that point on, Elizabeth seemed less edgy and overwhelmed. When worries came up, she was better at putting them aside. For the first time in her life, she was experiencing that rare and precious state we all wish for: peace of mind.

Peace of mind eludes almost everyone in the modern world because we look for it in the wrong place. We think it will come from some external accomplishment—enough money to retire on, a vacation home, a loyal spouse. But even if we achieve these goals, the peace of mind they give us is short-lived.

The reason is simple. In the material world, you're always vulnerable; whatever you gain you can also lose. The stock market can crash, a flood can wash away your home, your spouse can leave you. For peace of mind to be lasting, therefore, it must come from someplace where you are always nurtured and supported.

Lasting peace of mind can only come from a connection to the Source.

But for it to be really lasting, the connection has to be *ongoing*—which means you have to keep working on it. This is counterintuitive. Normally we envision peace of mind as a resting state. But that isn't peace, it's passivity. Because it requires constant work to stay connected to the Source—*peace of mind is an active state.*

This is a lot of work, but it's worth it. One benefit is a dramatic increase in energy and motivation. Most people have a faulty way of motivating themselves. They're motivated to get whatever they want—money, romance, status—because they feel they don't have enough already. This feeling of lack is a powerful motivator, but you pay a huge price for it. That price is the ongoing feeling that there's *always something missing.* Even if you get something you've wanted, you quickly become dissatisfied with it, which then motivates you to get something else. You can never be happy on this treadmill. Eventually, it sucks the meaning and energy out of your life.

The flaw in this way of motivating yourself is that you have to generate all the energy yourself. The alternative is to connect to an energy source much bigger than you, the true wellspring of all energy, the Source. You can't use the sense of something missing in order to plug into the Source. In fact, the more grateful you feel for what you already have, the more energy you get from it. Your gratitude opens the door to a completely new way of living in which the energy to move forward is based on happiness instead of misery.

Elizabeth's connection to the Source conferred another benefit on her. She discovered it when her daughter wasn't admitted to the college of her choice. "I started to freak out," she admitted, "but the Grateful Flow has become such a habit that I found myself using it almost without thinking. In the middle of this storm, I was able to find that calm, clear place. It was from there that I assured her: what mattered was not which college she went to, but how well she took advantage of its resources. I felt confident that she would do well in life no matter where she went to college, and I told her so. I could see how surprised she was that I wasn't the one who needed reassurance. It was a great feeling for both of us."

What Elizabeth had gained was that priceless quality we call *perspective*. Without perspective, any disappointment can take over your whole life; like a drop of ink in a beaker of water, *everything* looks dark. Even the smallest setback tends to overwhelm you. Perspective is the ability to see whatever is happening at the moment without losing sight of the enduring, positive nature of life. Only your connection to the Source gives you that awareness. When you have perspective, you can recover quickly from a disappointment because you see that your life is blessed by the Source.

Finally, an ongoing connection to the Source enables you to accept success. It may surprise you, but success can be paralyzing: a writer wins an Oscar and can't write for years afterward. Someone we know did an informal survey of physicists who won the Nobel Prize, and very few of them went on to accomplish any real breakthroughs after they won the award.

Success is paralyzing for a simple reason. It makes you feel as if you did it all yourself. Ironically, the moment you claim all the credit for your success, you also have to take the blame for any future failure—and that's terrifying. This makes you risk-averse, less creative, and afraid to move forward with new ideas and new projects. You rely on your past achievements, living a "safe," uncreative life.

The truth is, we accomplish nothing without the help of the Source. By acknowledging this, the Grateful Flow relieves you of total responsibility for what happens. You're free to take risks and be as creative as you can be.

The Grateful Flow is a direct acknowledgment of the Source as a co-creator in everything you achieve. Only this acknowledgment allows you to remain humble in the midst of success, which then enables you to remain creative for the rest of your life.

FREQUENTLY ASKED QUESTIONS

1. When I tried using the Grateful Flow, I couldn't feel the Source; in fact, I couldn't feel anything. What am I doing wrong?

It's quite common for people to use the Grateful Flow and not feel anything right away. For most of us, the organ of gratefulness is as useless as a foot that's gone to sleep. You have to exercise it before it works again. Similarly, you may have to use the Grateful Flow many times to awaken your sense of gratefulness. Only then will you be able to actually feel the Source.

Be patient with yourself. If your foot falls asleep, at least you *remember* what it's supposed to feel like. In contrast, you've never used gratefulness as an organ that senses the Source, so you'll have to both awaken it and get used to how it feels. Rest assured, gratefulness *is* a real organ—it exists inside of everyone. I've never met anyone who can't activate it if they try hard enough.

If all of this feels beyond you, just pick out five items you feel grateful for. Go slowly enough to fully feel your gratefulness for each item. That part of the tool alone will give you a potent weapon against negative thinking.

2. If I just focus on feeling grateful all the time, I'm afraid I'll ignore problems until it's too late to deal with them.

There are certainly people who live their whole lives with rose-colored glasses on, ignoring dangers until it's too late to deal with them. But these people have been like this their entire lives. In decades of teaching the Grateful Flow, we've never seen anyone develop these traits who didn't already have them.

Even if you *were* one of these naive people, we wouldn't recommend worry as a way of facing your problems. Most of us don't make the distinction between worrying and constructive problem solving. Constructive planning requires a calm and objective state, not out-of-control worry. You achieve that state only by staying connected to the Source. Besides, the Grateful Flow doesn't ignore the darkness, it just teaches you to see it as a blemish in a field of light. If you deny the darkness, you're ignorant. But if you can't see the light surrounding it, you're crippled.

And if you're still convinced you need your worries to keep you out of danger, here's a fail-safe exercise. Each morning, for a few minutes, write down all your fears, every danger you need to watch out for; everything that's a problem in your life that you're afraid you might forget. Now that all this is down on paper, you have no excuse—for the rest of the day, use the Grateful Flow. You'll be amazed at how well you can take care of yourself without the usual flood of dark worries.

3. If I become grateful for everything I already have, I'll get lazy; I won't have any motivation to make my life better.

This is another common objection to gratefulness. People are afraid they'll stop bettering themselves if they're content. *They're actually afraid to be happy.* Behind this objection lies a dark, pessimistic view of human beings: that we're lazy and can only be roused to move forward by threats to our survival. In essence, we're motivated by the adrenaline released when we're scared.

We don't deny that adrenaline is a powerful source of energy, but the problem is that it's a source of physical energy only. By its nature, *physical* energy is finite. Once it's used up, you become exhausted and depleted. This was Elizabeth's problem when I met her—just getting through an ordinary day had become a trial.

There's another problem when you rely on adrenaline to energize yourself: it distorts your perspective. You see events in life-and-death terms. In order to keep stimulating your adrenal glands, you're forced to seek increasingly risky situations. This leads to all kinds of bad decisions.

Wouldn't it be better if there were an energy system that kept you motivated without the drama; where you didn't need to see each event as a matter of life and death? Then you could be happy and motivated at the same time. For most of us, that state seems impossible. But it isn't. An infinite supply of energy is available to you at all times. It doesn't come from your body—it comes directly from the Source. And the key to connecting to the Source is the Grateful Flow.

4. When you say the Source cares about us and is always working on our behalf, you make it sound like the Source has human qualities. Is that a realistic way to think about it?

We've already said, but it's worth repeating, that the nature of the Source is far beyond human comprehension. But we don't have to fully understand it to relate to it. Attributing human qualities to the Source triggers emotions in us that make the relationship feel real. All religions, in their own way, personify the divine to reach the same end.

We've tried to describe the power of this relationship without implying that it's necessary to believe in any particular philosophy or theology. Ultimately, we don't care how you characterize the Source—what's most crucial is that you experience a connection with it. When you do, you'll feel supported and encouraged by something infinitely bigger than yourself; something that will grant you renewed strength when it seems like you have nothing left.

5. What about all the painful things that happen to us? Does the Source cause those things, too? And if so, doesn't that mean it *isn't* always working for our welfare?

The Source *is* always working to help us, but it often doesn't feel that way. The Source sees in us the limitless potential to create new things. With this creative power, we can reshape the world. But the human ego misunderstands this power. It sees creation only in terms of proving its own importance. To maintain that illusion, it claims that it creates everything on its own, without help; it denies that the Source even exists.

That isn't just wrong, it prevents us from ever fulfilling our potential. We do have the ability to create without end, but *we create nothing alone*. Each new thing humans bring to the world—everything from a new baby to a new technology—is done using the infinite energy of the Source. Our future potential doesn't lie in doing everything ourselves, it lies in the ability to co-create with the Source.

The Source is relentless in forcing us to realize this potential. It does this by destroying our illusion that we're the masters of the universe—and the go-it-alone mentality that comes with it. It doesn't do this with logic, *it does it with events.* It brings events into our lives that we don't want and can't control: illness, failure, rejection. The pain of these events brings us to our knees, forcing us to admit we're not the most powerful force in the universe. This is a blessing. It opens us up to our true higher potential—our partnership with the Source.

This reveals the hidden, higher meaning of adversity. Behind even the worst events, the Source is working for our welfare. When I explain this to my patients, they want to believe it. But as soon as things get really tough, they lose any sense that their pain has meaning. All they feel is that they're being unfairly punished. At this point, I encourage them to look outside themselves. If they do, they'll see an endless number of human beings suffering even worse adversity; and among them will always be some who aren't crushed by life, who remain buoyant and good-natured. These people seem to have an extraordinary ability to enjoy life and to radiate goodwill. Adversity hasn't dimmed their inner life—it has made it stronger.

This group senses the real purpose of adversity. Instead of resisting fate, they allow it to break down their egos. Consequently, as things get worse, their connection to the Source gets stronger. They radiate light in the darkest circumstances. And there has been no darker circumstance than that which Viktor Frankl described in his masterpiece, *Man's Search for Meaning* (which we referred to in Chapter 2). As you remember, he was a physician imprisoned in four different concentration camps during the Holocaust. Stripped of his position, family, and possessions, his life threatened on a daily basis, he set himself a goal of finding a sense of higher purpose in his situation. His success created a beacon of higher meaning that inspired those around him.

6. You say that worrying is a superstitious attempt to control the universe. Isn't that kind of grandiosity the mark of a narcissist?

Some habits are so universal that to call them narcissistic strains the definition of the word. Technically, narcissists are grandiose, need constant admiration, and have no empathy for others. The term is meant to describe a very specific group of people. Although a worrier hopes to control the world, it's not in a grandiose sense, nor do they look for any admiration in doing so. They're just trying to keep their head above water.

There's almost no one—from the most boastful to the most self-effacing—who doesn't succumb to worry. Deep down inside, we all fear that the universe is far beyond our control. And in a very primal way, we take refuge in the only activity that seems to offer a sense of power—thinking. The paradox is that it's exactly then that our thoughts spiral into uncontrollable worry.

We can find peace only when we accept the Source as the author of the events in our lives. When we become grandiose, that's the real way to put ourselves back into proper perspective.

7. Can I think of the Source as God?

The answer is you can, but you don't have to. We've intentionally defined the Source in a way that doesn't contradict the beliefs of any religion. This leaves our religious patients free to identify the Source as God. We've found that however they understand God, the Grateful Flow will work to dispel negative thinking.

On the other hand, there is a large group of people who have spiritual inclinations but don't connect easily to organized religion. For them, the concept of the Source gives a name to an experience they've already had but might not have defined: the sense that everything is given by a beneficent universe. This new focus deepens their sense of gratefulness and the relief from negativity that comes with it.

There's one group you'd expect to reject the idea of the Source—simply because it's affiliated with God: atheists. But atheism is a product of conscious thought. No matter what a person consciously believes, his unconscious sees the world in its own way. Carl Jung brilliantly revealed this in his study of dreams, religious imagery, and mythology. The unconscious lives in a world of universal symbols more powerful than logic. The Source is one of those symbols. When an atheist uses the Grateful Flow, his unconscious experiences the universe as all-giving, and that's all he needs to achieve peace of mind.

OTHER USES OF THE GRATEFUL FLOW

Some people don't worry as Elizabeth did. But that doesn't mean they can't benefit from using the Grateful Flow. There are other types of negative thinking, and the Grateful Flow works with all of them. Below, I describe three patients, each of whom demonstrates a different kind of negative thinking. In each case, they were able to use the Grateful Flow to dispel these thoughts. Much to their surprise, the tool freed them from limitations they'd imposed on themselves their whole lives.

The Grateful Flow frees you from regrets about the past. *Many of us fall into the habit of rethinking past decisions we've made, blaming those decisions for everything bad that's happened since. Besides the fact that life isn't that simple, this kind of regret makes it impossible to move forward into the future. You need a tool that allows you a renewed sense of possibilities right now; only then can you leave the past behind you.*

John was a divorced, middle-aged man who was stuck in the past. When he was younger, he had a series of relationships that he ended the moment he began to feel vulnerable. "As soon as I felt pressured, I'd bail," he said. He looked back at his decisions with regret, convinced he'd let the best women slip through his fingers. Now, in middle age, he wanted to date again, but the constant regret about the past made him feel like he'd used up all his chances. He'd lost all sense that he'd ever be in a relationship again. By the time he came to me for psychotherapy, he was chronically depressed.

I told him his past mistakes would have a bearing on the future only if he kept obsessing about them. His assignment was to use the Grateful Flow the moment he started to replay his past relationships. The tool did more than interrupt the stream of regrets. By reconnecting him to the Source, the future was once again filled with possibilities. As a part of that future, he could now see himself in a relationship with someone new. His renewed hope gave him the courage to date again.

The Grateful Flow frees you from self-hatred. *Self-hatred rarely has anything to do with your actual value as a person. It's the direct result of a stream of negative thoughts about yourself. Usually, these take the form of criticisms delivered by a harsh inner voice. This inner critic speaks with such authority that there's no reasoning with it. You need a tool that silences its voice altogether.*

Janet was a recent graduate of a top college who'd moved to Los Angeles to be with her boyfriend. He was one of those loser guys, but she was inexplicably attracted to him. He'd humiliate her in public by flirting with other women; he didn't contribute financially; he'd even leave her for weeks at a time. She reacted to these indignities by criticizing herself, as if everything were her fault. She wasn't understanding enough of him, she wasn't cool enough, or pretty enough. The worse he treated her, the worse these self-attacks became.

She expected me to dissuade her of these harsh judgments. She was surprised when I said we weren't going to argue with this inner critic, we were going to turn it off. She trained herself to use the Grateful Flow the moment she began to attack herself. Quickly, she began to develop a relationship with the Source. For the first time ever, she felt she was living in a universe that supported and valued her. The more she had this experience, the less accurate the self-criticisms seemed. Once she'd achieved this, she found the strength to stand up to her boyfriend and eventually leave him.

If you're a careful reader, you may have noticed that the issue of self-criticism is also dealt with in Chapter 4. There, we described self-criticism as an attack on the Shadow. Therefore, the tool we taught you—Inner Authority— emphasized accepting your Shadow. Here, we're describing self-criticism as a type of Black Cloud thinking. That's why, in this chapter, we're teaching you a tool that directly addresses your thoughts.

Over time, you'll find many problems that can be addressed through the use of more than one tool. In fact, our patients have had great success using two or even three tools for a given problem. Use your instincts; you'll find the best combination for you.

The Grateful Flow stops you from being judgmental about others. *When we judge others, we kid ourselves that what we think privately has no effect on those around us. The truth is that judgments, especially repeated harsh judgments, send an energy into the world that alienates others. You can't fake a nonjudgmental attitude; you actually have to eliminate the judgments themselves.*

George was a film director who, while still in his twenties, made two critically acclaimed films. Early success went to his head. He began to judge everyone he worked with—actors, crew members, even producers and executives from the studios that were funding his movies—finding them intellectually and creatively inferior. The result was a condescending attitude, which made people not want to work with him. His third film did poorly, and his career tanked. He became even more critical of others. By the time I met him, he hadn't received an offer of work in over a year. He felt completely demoralized.

He knew he had to stop judging people, but his sense

that he was "right" made it hard to stop. I told him it didn't matter whether his judgments were right or wrong; whenever he became judgmental, he was hurting himself. His negative judgments created his version of the Black Cloud. Cut off from the Source, he literally had nothing to offer those around him. Why would anybody want to work with him? I trained him to use the Grateful Flow the moment he began to judge anyone. This did more than interrupt his negativity. It gave him an immediate connection to the Source and its overflowing energy, which transformed his relationship with everyone. People found themselves getting more from him; they were inspired to give more to him.

SUMMARY OF GRATEFUL FLOW

What the Tool Is For

When your mind is filled with worry, self-hatred, or any other form of negative thinking, you've been taken over by the Black Cloud. It limits what you can do with your life, deprives your loved ones of what is best about you. Life becomes a struggle to survive instead of the fulfillment of great promise.

What You're Fighting Against

The unconscious delusion that negative thoughts can control the universe. Because we think the universe is indifferent to us, we cling to the sense of control negative thinking gives us.

Cues to Use the Tool

1. Use the Grateful Flow immediately whenever you are attacked by negative thoughts. If unchallenged, negative thinking will just get stronger.
2. Use the Grateful Flow any time your mind becomes undirected—when you're on "hold" during a phone call, stuck in traffic, or standing in line at the market.
3. You can even make the tool part of your daily schedule. That turns specific times (waking up, going to sleep, mealtimes) into cues.

The Tool in Brief

1. Start by silently stating to yourself specific things in your life you're grateful for, particularly items you'd normally take for granted. You can also include bad things that aren't happening. Go slowly so you really *feel* the gratefulness for each item. Don't use the same items each time you use the tool. You should feel a slight strain from having to come up with new ideas.

2. After about thirty seconds, stop thinking and focus on the physical sensation of gratefulness. You'll feel it coming directly from your heart. This energy you are giving out is the Grateful Flow.

3. As this energy emanates from your heart, your chest will soften and open. In this state you will feel an overwhelming presence approach you, filled with the power of infinite giving. You've made a connection to the Source.

The Higher Force You're Using

Far from being indifferent to us, there's a higher force in the universe that created us and remains intimately involved with our well-being. We call that higher force the Source. The experience of its overwhelming power dissolves all negativity. But without Gratefulness, we can't perceive the Source.

CHAPTER 6

The Tool:
Jeopardy

The Higher Force:
Willpower

THIS BOOK PUTS A SPECIAL POWER IN YOUR hands—the power to change your life. There's only one thing you need to do—*use the tools*. As a reward for doing this, you'll discover a better and newer version of yourself. Who doesn't want that?

I certainly assumed my patients did. The tools I gave them worked as promised; they became more confident and creative, more expressive and courageous. The results were so good, I was completely shocked by what happened next: almost every patient stopped using them. I was stupefied. I'd shown my patients the path to a new life and, for no good reason, they'd stepped off it—even the most enthusiastic ones quit.

Don't assume you'll do any better. My patients had a

big advantage over you. They had me hounding them every week like a personal trainer. Without that, you're even more likely to stop using the tools.

This needn't discourage you. Phil and I have since developed a way to keep you from quitting. But you have to understand that you're up against a formidable adversary. By the end of this chapter, you'll understand its tactics—and you'll be able to fight back.

Most self-help books don't even deal with the issue of quitting. They may give you a program, but they're unrealistic about how hard it will be to stick to it. We don't want to soft-pedal the challenge of changing your life—and we don't have to. That's because we can make you strong enough to pass the test.

The quickest way to start is to observe what happened to a patient of mine. You've already been introduced to him.

Remember Vinny? He was the stand-up comic who was so scared of pain he hid in the minor leagues of comedy. You can refresh your memory with a quick peek at Chapter 2. Full disclosure: when I wrote that chapter I left out certain parts of his story—dark moments when all progress stopped, when he was close to quitting altogether. If I had included these setbacks, the chapter would have been three times as long. But you need to understand the struggle he went through because you're going to go through your own version of it.

Vinny hated any kind of pain, but the kind he hated most was feeling vulnerable in front of others. That's why he avoided anyone with the power to help him. He wouldn't audition for them or even talk to them. He hid his fear with a mocking sense of humor that got old very quickly for those in his crosshairs.

Using the Reversal of Desire, he learned to conquer his pain avoidance. He began to show up to meetings on time, prepared and respectful. Soon he had business relationships with people who had the power to help him; they put him in the top clubs. Then he got the chance to audition for a new TV sitcom that had a lot of buzz. This was his greatest dream. But, because it made him feel vulnerable, it was also his worst fear.

He had to go through a high-pressure series of auditions, but he used the Reversal of Desire with even more discipline. It let him overcome his fear and—to his own surprise—he got the part. Now he had a bridge to the future he wanted; all he had to do was cross it. If his fear returned, he had the Reversal of Desire to keep him on track.

A few days after he got the part, I saw him in my office. Within minutes, it was clear he wasn't going to cross the bridge—he was going to jump off it. I told him he was going to need a realistic plan to deal with the pressures of his new situation. He didn't seem to hear me; instead he launched into a self-satisfied rant about all the celebs he was meeting and how funny they thought he was. I had the distinct feeling Vinny had left reality for a magical world where all his wishes could come true.

Alarm bells started going off in my head. "Vinny, this is the point where people self-destruct. At the first taste of success, they stop working on themselves. But reality hasn't changed. They need the tools even more than before."

"Doc," he shot back coldly, "I'm gonna be a star. Have you seen how the world treats stars? I'm on easy street from now on."

After working with celebrities for years, I knew how ridiculous this was. To name a few of their problems, there were broken relationships, trouble with their kids, illness, stalkers, aging, bad reviews, and thieving business managers. The smart ones knew success wouldn't protect them. They worked hard in therapy, especially with the tools.

Vinny wasn't one of the smart ones. He needed an example of a problem he could relate to. "How about if one of the scripts is written so your character isn't funny? Remember, millions will be watching."

He waved his hand dismissively. "I'm too important to the show for them to make me look bad. There are two articles coming out on me next month!" Vinny had no idea how expendable he really was.

Happily ignorant, he made his life into a nonstop celebration of his delusions. His first official act was to stop using the Reversal of Desire. This was the equivalent of the Lone Ranger shooting his faithful horse, Silver. Without the Reversal of Desire, Vinny's newfound adult habits slipped away. The person who worked on his material daily, exercised, and lived in a clean house was nowhere to be found.

Not that the house went unused—his old posse of sycophants gathered there nightly. High on pot, beer, and cheap adulation he re-created his Comfort Zone. Sometimes he'd invite a D-level celeb to stop by to add some "class" to the proceedings (which just shows how high he was).

But he still had a show to do. The woman who ran the sitcom had the inexplicable habit of wanting the actors to say the words she'd written in the script. Which meant learning them. Vinny complained about this. "What's the big deal if I improvise? That's what I do for a living. If she wasn't such a hack, she'd take advantage of it."

It wasn't the "hack's" problem, it was Vinny's. Memorizing lines was no fun—he saw it as one more thing a star was excused from. His boss wasn't sympathetic; when Vinny showed up hungover and tried to ad-lib a whole scene, she read him the riot act.

Things went downhill from there. He began to show up late to work; when he was there, he was nasty and uncooperative, and the other actors started to shun him. I warned him things would come to a bad end if he didn't grow up—and start using the Reversal of Desire. This caused some friction between us (if you consider his screaming at me that I was a loser friction). He began to miss our sessions and finally quit therapy. There was nothing I could do about this; he'd stopped listening to me a long time ago.

DO YOU BELIEVE IN MAGIC?

It was obvious Vinny had quit on himself. In a less blatant way, most of my other patients did the same thing.

They may have stayed in therapy, but like Vinny, they convinced themselves it was okay to stop using the tools. It wasn't—they were sabotaging themselves just like he was. I can confidently predict that you're going to find yourself in the exact same boat. You'll try the tools, love what they do for you, and yet you'll stop using them.

How can this be so widespread? The answer is that our entire culture has an unreal view of what it means to be human. We like to think of ourselves as finished products—complete on our own. We're not. To be whole, we need to stay connected to something beyond ourselves. The constant effort that requires means that a human being can never be more than a work in progress.

Think of your mind as a newly bought, state-of-the-art, flat-screen TV. You eagerly take it out of the box, but it won't play. An electrical connection has come loose; there's no buying a new connection, you have to fix it with your own effort. Worse, the connection will keep coming loose—you'll have to fix it every day. But the broken connection in your mind isn't to electrical power, it's to higher forces. And every time the connection breaks, one of your personal problems appears. The tools repair the connection—that's why they work. But the connection never lasts; it will break again.

That makes using tools a task without end.

This is humbling. Not only isn't it our choice, it's something we'll have to do for the rest of our lives. One of my patients was a great example of how hard this is to accept. A few weeks after she moved into her newly constructed dream house, she came to my office crying bitterly. She already hated her kitchen, but not in the way you'd think. Every night after dinner, she'd scrub the dishes and counters spotless. "The moment I finish, I get into this rage. Before you know it, my husband's going to be down there leaving crumbs from a late-night snack. Tomorrow morning my two-year-old is going to fling her applesauce against the wall. Why did I even bother to clean up? It never stays that way."

But what if there were a way to free her from the endless drudgery? This might sound like a pitch on a late-night infomercial, except that it's serious. Every one of us has a fantasy of a "magical something"—a relationship, job, achievement, or possession—that will remove us from the treadmill that is real life. Applied to housework, it might be the fantasy of a self-cleaning kitchen. But applied to human beings, it's the fantasy that we'd stop needing higher forces to complete ourselves. Then we wouldn't need tools at all.

For Vinny the "magical something" was fame. Now he had it, so the need to face pain was over. In fact, struggle of any kind should be over. If Vinny had a religion, this was it. He didn't seek Heaven, just easy street. In his own words: "I've wanted this since I was a kid getting beaten by my father for having a dream. I've done my part—now I get the reward."

The reward has a name. Phil calls this fantasy of living an effort-free, undemanding life "exoneration." Most people think of exoneration in terms of being cleared of a crime, but it has another meaning: to be excused from a task or obligation. Here, it refers to the ultimate obligation—to make an effort for the rest of your life.

Deep down, we all wish for a magical something that will exonerate us. It could be money, an award, a high-achieving child, looking cool in front of your friends, etc. Take a moment and identify what it is for you. It doesn't matter what it is, it could be the smallest thing; just be honest with yourself. Then, try the following exercise:

> Let yourself fantasize that you get the "magical something" and it does take the struggle out of your life. Let yourself feel that for a moment. Now, crush that fantasy: imagine it can never become reality. How does it feel knowing you can never escape life's endless struggles?

Now you know why almost every patient quit using the tools. It wasn't enough that their lives were improving in every way. They wanted what the tools could never bring them—a magic pill to exonerate them from the struggle. Spiritually, they were still children.

THE PRICE OF EXONERATION

There's a penalty for spiritual immaturity.

After Vinny quit therapy, I didn't see him for several months. Then, returning from lunch one day, I stepped out of the elevator on my floor and someone grabbed me. At first, I thought I was being mugged, but I quickly realized I was being held on to for dear life. Then I heard the sobs.

It was Vinny as I'd never seen him before; face bright red, bloodshot eyes, tears streaming. He looked at me with a soul-penetrating gaze I'll never forget, but he couldn't get any words out. I led him into the office and locked the door behind us.

"They fired me." He gave me that look again. "Why didn't I listen to you?"

I told him that we needed to get to work, that what he was going through now was just another kind of pain and the Reversal of Desire would still work. (See Chapter 2 to review how this tool works on events that have already happened.) I sent him home to clean up, with instructions to use the tool over and over until I could see him.

The next time I saw him, he was a bit better, but he hadn't used the Reversal of Desire even once. "Vinny, time is crucial here. I'm trying to save you from the ultimate penalty."

"You already lost that one, Doc."

Vinny thought that the greatest cost was to his career. It was true that in a very short time he'd gone from being a promising comedic actor—with a perfect platform to advance his career—to an unemployable pariah. It was a spectacular fall. But when I pressed him again on using the Reversal of Desire, his response revealed the ultimate penalty.

"You don't get it, Doc, I can barely get outta bed."

Vinny had fallen into a black pit. Only the tools could help him climb out, but he was too demoralized to use them. Losing his job was just one, outer event. But the real damage happens when we get permanently demoralized and stop trying. That's when we've lost everything: we have no future.

I was intimately acquainted with demoralization. Just like Vinny, I'd been betrayed by my own magical plan. When I was ten years old, I started working like a beast with the goal of getting into Harvard College. I took as many honors and advanced placement courses as I could—in fact, I worked so hard I not only got into Harvard, they allowed me to skip my freshman year. I was elated. But when I arrived in Cambridge and realized the truth—I had even more work to do—I crashed. I barely passed my first year.

Out entire culture is demoralized. All the symptoms are there: we delight in the adrenal rush of cheap sex and petty violence; we avoid real problem solving in favor of scoring points against our opponents. We've lost hope in our future. That's the ultimate price for indulging childish fantasies.

Exoneration is impossible—for an individual or for a society. When, inevitably, this false hope for "easy street" is shattered, we're left demoralized. This is an inescapable law: *exoneration always ends in demoralization.*

There's a path that can lead us out of this mess. But we

have an enemy that's dead set against us taking it. It attacks us every waking moment: when we turn on the TV, go on the Internet, or read a magazine; it gets to us even while we're driving, and especially when we enter the dark, inner sanctum of its power, the shopping mall.

FANTASY FOR SALE

The enemy is called "consumerism." It speaks to us through every advertisement, endorsement, logo, roadside billboard, etc. Its underlying message is always the same: there's something out there you must have. Helpless to resist, we feel compelled to acquire thing after thing. Yet we don't enjoy each new item for long; once we possess it, we shift our focus to the next thing.

Inevitably, consumerism insinuates itself into all of our activities, not just shopping. We consume life experiences the same way we consume iPods, jeans, and European cars. A given song, idea, or friend is new and different until it's not. Then we discard it and go on to the next thing. Consumerism has become our model for living. This is the tail wagging the dog.

He didn't like admitting it, but Vinny got wagged as much as the next person. When he did use the tools, his goal was external—to become famous. They were a crutch he needed until he got there; then he discarded them.

You're no more immune from consumerism than Vinny was. You're probably in its grip right now. If you don't believe this, take an honest look at how you're reading this book. As a consumer, you'll read it quickly and superficially, hoping it is the "answer" you've been seeking. You'll want the book to work like a pill, even if you don't admit it; just swallow, no further effort required.

This book is designed to change your life. But it's not a magic pill, it's a blueprint for action. If you read it like a consumer, you might as well not read it at all. Change only happens through the faithful use of the tools. You might read something that inspires you to use them, but your resolve will fade quickly and you'll quit. It's like the old joke "When I feel the urge to work, I lie down 'til it passes." Only it's not funny.

Consumers try to make up for their laziness by gorging on new information—TV, podcasts, web searches, texts, e-mails, etc. But like a meal eaten too quickly, nothing is really digested. I once met a woman at a seminar who told me she'd read seventy-five books on spirituality in the past month. How could she find meaning in one book when she was already consuming the next? Trying to consume spirituality is like buying multiple GPS systems for your car and not learning to use any of them.

As obvious as the presence of consumerism is in our lives, we still can't resist it. Its power is actually based on something healthy. We have a natural desire for a relationship with higher forces that's so strong it can never be eradicated. Consumerism misdirects that desire by convincing you that higher forces exist *inside* the magical something.

That way, once you obtain it, you *own* the higher forces; you don't need a relationship with them. This "treasure hunt" is a quest for the impossible, but rather than admitting that, we relentlessly search for the next magical something.

The misdirected search for magic surrounds you every day. Consumers might deny this, but it shows in their behavior. They pursue something—a new spouse, a new wardrobe, a new hobby—with tremendous expectation. The expectation is never met, and that just makes them search even harder. Next time you see a sharp-elbowed group of shoppers frantically burrowing through the sale items at a department store, tell yourself you're witnessing a hunt for cosmic magic. That should keep you away from sales for a while.

But you're not really free until all hope for magic is crushed.

THE HIGHER FORCE: WILLPOWER

It's no fun to have your hope crushed. It took Vinny a while to see it as anything but a disaster. For the first month after he came back to therapy, every session was a combination of a fight and a pep talk. I had to convince him that the only way back to the living was by connecting to higher forces—and then staying connected. There would never be a time when he was finished using the tools. When he first grasped this, he sat there as if he'd been given a life sentence. I tried to engage him.

"What are you thinking, Vinny?"

"I used to look forward to having my own show, now there's nothing in my future besides using the tools."

"That's a good first step. A month ago you thought you had no future."

Vinny eventually came to believe that this humble process was the only way to save himself. (I certainly told him that often enough.) But there were still times—plenty of them—when he couldn't get himself to use the tools. What had changed was that now he *wanted* to use them—which only made him feel more hopeless when he couldn't. This is a disorienting experience for most people. We like to think that we have rational control over ourselves; that once we decide we need to do something, we can do it.

Vinny was forced to admit that taking action wasn't so simple. "I can't follow my own directions. Something is missing. . . . I hope you know what it is," he said shakily.

I did. But I wanted him to *feel* the answer. "What's the greatest comeback you've ever seen?"

"It was a boxing match. Does that count?"

"Perfect. What happened?"

"This guy was fighting above his weight class, but he was holding his own. In the last round, he took a tremendous shot to the chin. He was lying on the canvas like he was dead. I know it sounds crazy, but after a six count he suddenly came back to life. It was like he flipped a switch. The son of a bitch actually got up and finished the fight. He fought to a draw; it was the greatest fight I ever saw."

"Okay. Close your eyes and imagine the moment when he flipped that switch. What do you see happening inside him?"

"Everything was dark. All of a sudden, there's this spark."

"You just saw what you're missing."

"That's it? That's what's gonna save me? A fucking spark?"

"That 'fucking spark' is the only thing that can save you. It brought that fighter back from the dead. You know what we call it?" For a change, Vinny was silent. "It's called willpower."

That wasn't the revelation Vinny was hoping for. He reacted like he'd just paid full price for a fake Rolex. But like most people, Vinny's view of willpower was shaped in the third grade. He had no idea what real willpower was, let alone how to develop it.

It's a rare individual who feels she couldn't use more of it—usually much more. We call on willpower when we have to do something difficult or unpleasant: working out, balancing a checkbook, even getting up in the morning. Or we call on it when we need to restrain harmful impulses such as overeating or drug use.

These are situations where the world around you is of no help—in fact, you have to act despite it. You need a force you can generate completely from inside yourself. Western culture represents it as a light appearing in the darkness, as if out of nowhere. That was the spark Vinny saw.

When Vinny "couldn't follow his own directions" to use the tools, what was missing was the spark of willpower. Without it, he'd end up quitting again—the therapy would be a failure. Because this was true for so many of our patients, we developed a way to strengthen their willpower. Anyone—even those most prone to giving up—can develop a degree of willpower they didn't think possible.

Very few models of human growth accept this, let alone give you a way to build your willpower. Instead, they pretend it's easy to change your life. It isn't. Our approach is the opposite: we're telling you the truth about how difficult it's going to be—and we're going to make you strong enough to face the challenge. Doing that means increasing your willpower—which is what the fifth tool does. In a sense it's the most important one—the tool that makes sure you keep using the other tools. It won't matter how effective the other four are if you don't use them.

As a reader you might sense a contradiction here. The four tools we've presented so far draw their extraordinary power from the fact that they reach out to higher forces that are already present. But we've defined willpower as something that's not there unless you generate it yourself. Can it still be a higher force? It can, but there's something about it that's different from the four we've already described.

Those four are given to us as gifts. Willpower isn't. Human beings participate in its creation. The universe is involved, but only to provide the context in which human beings develop willpower. In terms of Vinny's image of the fighter, the universe contributed the darkness. Fortunately, most of us aren't boxers lying on a canvas. Our darkness comes at those moments when we're completely demoralized and want to give up.

We rarely understand what a gift the darkness is. Without it, there would be no way to discover our own inner spark. It's exactly when we're demoralized that the universe becomes our partner. Demoralization is actually our most sacred moment.

But only if we know what to do with it. That's why we need a fifth tool.

THE TOOL: JEOPARDY

In effect, we need a tool that generates the spark of willpower that got the boxer off the canvas and that you will need to get through your darkest moments of demoralization. That spark is more than the resolution to do something in the future (just look back at your last New Year's resolutions). The tool must move you to act right now. The choice is black or white: you either use the tools or you don't.

To act right now requires a sense of urgency. But urgency is uncomfortable. The only time we feel it is when we're in jeopardy of losing something important: a job, a relationship, physical safety. An upcoming recital might put a musician's reputation in jeopardy, so she practices twice as much. A business presentation might put an executive's promotion at stake, so he stays up all night preparing. From here on—for the sake of brevity—we'll call this kind of situation simply "jeopardy." It triggers a burst of energy you can't get any other way.

I had an unforgettable lesson in the power of jeopardy while studying for the California bar exam. The test is a three-day ordeal. More than half the candidates fail; I didn't want to be one of them. For months, I did nothing but study, empty pizza boxes piling up around me. It was the most alert and focused I'd ever been. I lived in fear (terror would be more accurate) that I'd be brought down by some obscure part of the law I'd neglected to cover. Every moment felt crucial. I remember thinking that if I could concentrate like this all the time, there'd be nothing I couldn't do.

The strength I was feeling came to me because—for the first time in my life—I had accepted that time is limited. I couldn't afford to waste it ruminating about the past or fantasizing about the future. The only thing that mattered was what I was doing at that moment.

For most of us, the truth—that every moment counts—is too much pressure to bear. It would mean giving our all, all of the time. We prefer to stay comfortable until a deadline forces us to act. But deadlines pass and the willpower they trigger goes away. As soon as my bar exam was over, so was my sense of jeopardy. I returned to my usual passive way of life, partying every night until I fell into a depression. Like most people, I took this as the way of the world.

When I met Phil, he convinced me that there was a better way. He said something that had never occurred to me. "Real willpower can't be dependent on events, willpower has to be beyond events."

That was confusing. "Isn't it events that put you in jeopardy?"

"Events are temporary. You need to find a permanent source of jeopardy. There's only one thing you're at risk of losing every moment."

"What is it?"

"Your future."

Most people don't think of the future as something that's theirs to lose. But that changes if you use the tools regularly. Not only does this enable you to overcome your problems in the present, it changes who you become in the future. Whether you're a novelist, an entrepreneur, or a parent, you become capable in a way you never were before. You become a party to the shaping of your own future. With access to higher forces, your potential has no limits.

If you keep using the tools, this limitless potential is your future. But the benefit is not automatic. All you have to do is stop using them and your potential is destroyed. That raises the stakes. Your future is in jeopardy every moment. That generates tremendous urgency—and the willpower that comes with it. The penalty for not using the tools is much greater than we'd like to admit. With Vinny, I wanted him to feel how severe that penalty could be.

I had him close his eyes and imagine that, defeated by

his own demoralization, he never used the tools again. "What would your life look like after a few years?"

An image came up immediately—it made him grimace. "I'm this decrepit, three-hundred-pound piece of shit, lying in a bed that hasn't been made since prehistoric times.... My God!" Something had terrified him. "I'm living in my mother's house!"

This wasn't funny to Vinny—it was a humiliating disaster. He couldn't resort to his old trick of blaming bad news on me; the image emerged from his unconscious completely on its own. For the first time in his life, Vinny saw what was at stake. It didn't matter what came out of his mouth; only action could save him—he either used the tools or didn't.

Each person has his own version of a destroyed future. Whatever it is for you, the pain and regret it causes is enormous. To keep yourself from quitting on the tools, you'll need a way to stay aware of how much is at stake. That's what the fifth tool does. It's this awareness that creates the urgency that triggers unwavering willpower.

Because the tool is based on the risk of losing your future, we call it "Jeopardy." When we use the word with a capital *J* it refers to the tool. In some ways, it's the most important one—it's your insurance policy against quitting on the other four tools.

To understand how Jeopardy works, pick out one of the basic tools from Chapters 2–5—one that seems most important for your own growth. Then, read the whole Jeopardy tool carefully before you try it on your own.

Jeopardy

Imagine you can see far into the future. See your-self lying on your deathbed. This older self knows how crucial the present moment is, because he's run out of them. You see him rouse himself from his bed and scream at you not to waste the present moment. You feel a deep, hidden fear that you've been squandering your life. This creates an urgent pressure to use—right now—the basic tool you selected above.

Some patients initially feel put off when asked to look at their last moment on earth. But this is the perspective that creates the greatest sense of urgency. Death is the most powerful reminder that there are only so many moments in a human life. That makes each present moment priceless. The galvanizing effect of a nearness to death was elo-quently described by the eighteenth-century British writer Samuel Johnson, who said, "When a man knows he is to be hanged in a fortnight, it concentrates his mind wonder-fully."

Unless you're currently on death row, this kind of in-exorable focal point is probably not part of your daily experience, which is convenient if you want to stay com-fortable. But beneath it all, most of us live with a hidden fear that we're wasting our lives. The unbelievable number of distractions consumerism offers helps us bury that fear. Using Jeopardy breaks through our denial and turns our fear into the urgency to act. That urgency lights the spark of willpower.

There is never a time when you don't need that spark. That's why Phil said we needed a "permanent source of jeopardy." The deathbed perspective provides it, regardless of your outer situation. It allows you to create willpower at any time.

The picture below shows the process of creating willpower.

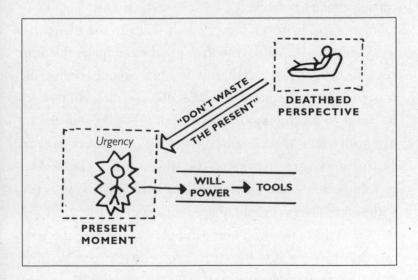

The figure at the upper right represents you lying on your deathbed. He's much more aware than you are that time is limited. His warning to you is symbolized by the arrow labeled, "Don't waste the present." The figure inside the box labeled "Present Moment" is you. The jagged lines surrounding you represent urgent pressure to use the present moment before it's gone. It's this urgency that creates the willpower to use the tools. As long as you remain aware of this warning, you'll have the will to use the tools over and over again. You're shaping a pathway to an expanded future.

WHEN TO USE JEOPARDY

Although Jeopardy is effective at any time, there are certain moments when it's most crucial. Identifying these moments will help you recognize the cues to use the tool.

Vinny has provided us with a great example of the first cue. He *wanted* to use the tools but he *couldn't*, because he was completely demoralized. We all have moments when we want to use the tools but just can't. We may not be as demoralized as he was; maybe we chalk it up to laziness or exhaustion. It doesn't matter. Once you find it impossible to use the tools, the only thing that can help you is extra willpower. That's the cue to use Jeopardy.

Vinny has also been kind enough to illustrate the second and less-obvious cue. It has to do with success. Like Vinny, we mistake success with being exonerated from further struggle. We tell ourselves we no longer need to exert willpower. But no matter how good we feel, if it becomes an excuse to quit using the tools, success destroys our future.

That defines the second cue. Any time we feel like we've grown beyond the need for the tools is an immediate cue to use Jeopardy.

Obviously, our tendency to quit isn't limited to the tools. We quit diets, exercise programs, writing self-help books, relationships, etc. In all of these situations what's needed is increased willpower. Jeopardy works just as well here as it does for getting yourself to use the tools. So consider this a third cue. Whenever you lose the will to go on in life areas that are important to you, Jeopardy is your friend.

Willpower is the missing link in reaching human potential. Because it's so crucial, you'll discover many other situations where you need it. Try out Jeopardy in those everyday moments when you tend to lose your will: getting out of bed in the morning, concentrating in the face of distractions, or restraining the impulse to give in to a bad habit. It works just as well at those heightened moments when you'd like to take your life in a new direction. You might want to start a book, a new business, or move to a new city. You fantasize about it endlessly but you don't even take step one. We'll elaborate on these other uses of Jeopardy at the end of this chapter.

Jeopardy is more than a tool. It's a model for being fully alive. Paradoxically, this sense of life emerges from a relationship with the deathbed version of yourself. Because he knows what it's like for time to run out, he has the wisdom you need every moment. Invite him into your consciousness, feel him looking at you every moment, and welcome the pressure he puts on you. You'll move through life with a wind at your back.

THE SECRET BENEFIT OF WILLPOWER

Vinny felt the first breeze as soon as he began using Jeopardy.

He burst into a session and told me he'd gone back to work. His gig was at a tiny club in Pasadena, but I'd never seen him more enthusiastic. "Something's different. I don't care that no big shots come, I don't even care how the audience reacts. Before, I would've done just enough to make it good and then kicked back. Now all I want to do is make it better and better."

The moment I heard this, I knew something important had happened. It was great that Vinny was working again, but this was change on a much more profound level. Vinny had taken his first giant step away from the superficial life of the consumer and into a whole new way of being. He had become a "creator."

The consumer expects a reward for the slightest effort—or better, for no effort at all. He cares only about what he gets from the world, not about what he might add to it. Living on the surface, jumping from thing to thing, his energy is diffused, like milk spreading across a tabletop. He makes no impact on the world; when his time on earth is over, it's as if he never lived.

The creator won't accept that fate. Everything he does is with the intention of making an impact on the world. His code ensures this:

> He doesn't accept the world as he finds it; he brings things into the world that aren't already there.

> He doesn't follow the herd; he sets his own course. He ignores the reactions of others.

> He resists superficial distractions. He remains focused on his goals even if he has to sacrifice his immediate gratification.

Anyone can live by this code, but very few of us do. It means putting your life in the service of higher forces. These forces can't be found on the surface of life; they're found in its depths. The creator's energy must have the singular focus of a drill boring through stone. As difficult as that is, a creator is rewarded many times over for his efforts.

You don't have to be an artist to be a creator. You can add something to the world in any human activity—even the most routine. Your job, your role as a parent, your relationships, your contribution to your community—all become more meaningful when you put your personal stamp on them using higher forces.

For Vinny, the sense that his life actually meant something was an unexpected gift. For the first time, he had a sense of purpose and the confidence that went with it. But he still doubted that he had what it took to live as a creator for the rest of his life. I told him everyone had the same doubt about themselves.

He wasn't easily reassured. "Why do they make this so hard?"

They? I was shocked by the question. Vinny never asked for spiritual explanations for anything. But I took it as progress; he was looking in the right place even if he'd never looked there before. To help him understand, I told him the following story. I'd heard it from a rabbi who studied Kabbalah. I can't vouch for its authenticity but it gets the point across:

An old rabbi was teaching his student about God's creation of the human race. God labored carefully to create man in His own image. When He was finished, He looked at His creation but was unsatisfied; He'd wanted to create a being he could relate to, a peer. But man was lacking one key attribute that God had—the ability to create. So God made the earth and placed man in its challenging environment. Man was forced to create—build shelter, raise crops, invent the wheel. Now man had all the attributes of God. The student was confused. "Why did God go to all this trouble?

Why not just give man creative powers?" The old
rabbi replied, "That is the one thing that cannot be
given."

Creative power can't be given because the act of creation is an expression of yourself, a revelation of who you
are inside. No one, not even God, can give this to you—*it
must come from you.* You have to develop creative powers
through your own efforts.

Vinny was suspicious. "Sounds like God's lame excuse
for not taking care of us."

When consumers say, "taking care of us," they really
mean exonerating us from the struggle. But the story explains that God's real "job" is to keep us *in the struggle.* This
view of God doesn't go down well when your ultimate goal
is a life of ease. I've found that even atheists reject it. (Just
in case there is a God, they want to make sure He serves
their false hopes.)

Or in Vinny's words, "Are you shitting me? You're saying God's job is to hold our feet to the fire and leave us to
rescue ourselves? If I'm ever in church again, I'm taking
money *out* of the collection box."

Vinny was right, we do have to rescue ourselves. But
the reward for doing that is more valuable than money.
It's the chance to live as a creator, the deepest, most meaningful experience we can have. If God did exonerate us,
He'd be taking that opportunity away from us. Human be-

ings are only happy when they are reaching toward their highest potential. Paracelsus, a Renaissance physician and mystic, put it this way: "Happiness does not consist in laziness. . . . In labour and in sweat must each man use the gifts that God conferred upon him on earth, . . ."

In modern terms, the rabbi's story was about God's need for man to become a creator. Only then, would God have a peer. That's why "they make it so hard." Our existence has to be difficult, or we never find our way to the potential God wants us to have.

The most immediate experience we can have of being a creator is when we use Jeopardy. The tool allows us to literally create willpower out of nothing. The spiritual model for creating something out of nothing is described in Genesis, where darkness reigned until God said, "Let there be light." In our lives, darkness reigns when we're demoralized and can't act. When we use Jeopardy to create the spark of willpower, we bring light into our personal universe the same way that God brought it to the cosmos.

This completely transforms the meaning of failure, demoralization, and paralysis. They all become opportunities for us to exercise a godlike creativity. If you can do this, you've marked yourself as a creator—independent of outer achievements. You become fearless. The future may bring you darkness, but it can't take away your ability to create light.

Using the tool confers yet another benefit—the best one of all. As Vinny became more committed to living as a creator, he continued to use Jeopardy whether he felt great or wanted to give up altogether. Within a few months, he realized he was experiencing something completely new to him.

He was happy.

The change was stunning from my perspective. When I looked into his eyes, I no longer saw a cynical, rebellious adolescent staring at me. In its place was a grown man whose heart was open to the world. And his worst fear hadn't come true: he was still funny. But now, instead of using humor as a weapon in a war against humanity, he gave it as a gift to make others happy—which made him happy.

Yet another shock was the way others were reacting to him. He found that the happier he was, the more people were drawn to him. The atmosphere in the club had become electric any night that he was performing. It was a heady experience for him. "They used to laugh because they knew I hated them. I gave that up and tried to love them—and they laughed even harder. And you know what? I like it much better."

He was outspoken in giving Jeopardy the credit for his transformation. "Doc, in a million years I would never have guessed the secret to happiness: just think about death all day." Vinny had condensed the last ten thousand years of spiritual wisdom into one joke. He had truly become a creator.

Once you aspire to become a creator, everything changes, even the way you read this book. We've already explained how a consumer will read it—quickly and superficially, scanning it for magical sources of power he can get without effort on his part.

A consumer will certainly get new insights and some great tools from the book. But we wrote it with a much more ambitious purpose in mind. We want to change your life—really change it, not just talk about it. We're convinced this is possible. But you have to read the book the way a creator would.

As a creator, you won't be looking for a temporary thrill or to be the first on your block with some new techniques. You'll read the book slowly and thoughtfully because you need the help of higher forces. You wouldn't dream of stopping the tools—you have things you want to do with the powers they give you. You want to have a real impact on the world, to add something new to it.

For a creator, what we've written becomes more than a book. It's a guide you'll return to over and over again, the way a builder uses a blueprint. But you aren't building a new house; you're building a new life.

For us, every reader is a potential creator. That possibility is what drives us as authors. We will not be satisfied if you read the whole book; we won't be satisfied if you use a few tools now and then; we won't even be satisfied if you find it inspirational and tell all your friends. We've succeeded only if you come away from it using the tools without end. Then you'll become a creator. That is our goal—and it should be yours, too.

FREQUENTLY ASKED QUESTIONS

1. I've been a member of Alcoholics Anonymous for fifteen years. AA teaches that "self-will run riot" lies at the core of our problem. Yet you seem to imply that willpower is the key to the solution. Which is right?

This is a matter of terminology. When AA uses the term *self-will*, they're referring to the delusion that the universe will conform to your expectations.

When we use the term *willpower*, it has nothing to do with controlling the universe. It's the very fact that we have no control that makes willpower so vital. The most obvious thing we have no control over is time—it's constantly slipping away. Jeopardy uses this to create a sense of urgency. Each time you use the tool, you're surrendering to time. The most direct way to experience this is from your imaginary deathbed. Death—determined by a power greater than any individual—is the ultimate loss of control. The willpower Jeopardy creates is thus in complete harmony with this Higher Power. It couldn't exist without it.

2. What do I do if I can't get myself to use the Jeopardy tool?

No matter how demoralized or lazy you are, if you're alive and conscious, you have enough energy to make some tiny effort on your own behalf. Even the most minuscule effort counts. For instance, maybe all you can do is see a picture of yourself on your deathbed. That takes less effort than it does to read this answer. Maybe the next time you can see the deathbed figure animated with some emotion. You can play with this, the way a child would. Before you know it, you'll surprise yourself by being able to use the tool. The only real mistake you can make is to do nothing.

3. I believe in positive visualization. It seems like the Jeopardy tool uses fear to motivate you. Isn't that the opposite of spiritual?

You're absolutely right that Jeopardy is based on fear. But that doesn't make it unspiritual. The tool forces you to be aware that your time here is limited, and your death will be a reality at some point. It's exactly that experience that awakens the deepest need for a spiritual connection. But, as should be obvious by now, that connection takes work. That's where fear comes in. It's hardwired into the primitive part of your brain that guards your survival. That part of you never quits, so it creates a kind of willpower that endures. On the other hand, if you rely on the promise of a feel-good philosophy to motivate you, when, inevitably, that promise isn't fulfilled, your willpower disappears.

4. I used one of the tools but I changed an element in it and it seemed to work better for me. Is that okay?

As we explained in Chapter 1, when Phil developed the tools, he subjected them to extensive testing to find the most effective version of each. That's why we recommend that, when you're learning them, you follow the directions closely. This ensures you'll create at least some connection to higher forces. If, over time, you find yourself changing them a bit, then, the change will be directed by the higher forces themselves.

But in the long run, the most important thing is that you keep using the tools. If you're more likely to do that by using your own version, go right ahead. Whatever version you do use, pay careful attention to the cues as we've laid them out. We've identified these cues on the basis of years of experience. Take them seriously, and of course, feel free to add your own.

The way you use the tools should be a step in the direction of creatorship. A creator values his own instincts and experiences above any set of arbitrary directions—even the ones we're giving to you. This doesn't mean you can't follow the tools as written; in fact, for many people that's what works best. What's most important is that you find a way of weaving them into the fabric of your life that's meaningful to you.

OTHER USES

In this chapter, we've focused on the use of Jeopardy to fulfill the mission of this book—getting you to use the first four tools. That requires willpower, and Jeopardy will deliver it for you. But willpower is so crucial that you'll find Jeopardy indispensable in many other circumstances. Here are three of the most common.

Jeopardy supplies you with the willpower to control addictive and impulsive behavior. *We have much less control over ourselves than we'd like to think. Whether it's what we eat, what we buy, or how we react to other people, etc., we can't resist the pull of immediate gratification. We resolve repeatedly to change our behavior, but impulses always win in the end. What we need isn't more resolutions; it's a way to defeat our impulses right in the moment. That takes willpower.*

Ann was the picture of the well-adjusted wife and mother. But when it came to shopping, she became a different person. She'd go on the Internet with the intention of answering e-mails and entering in calendar items. At some point, she'd "feel the itch." A magnetic force would draw her to her extensive list of shopping sites. She'd tell herself she'd only look for five minutes and then get back to work, but those were just words. Hypnotized by the world of electronic shopping, she'd lose all track of time and never seemed to escape without at least one unnecessary purchase. When it was over, she'd be overtaken by guilt and exhaustion, as if she'd had illicit sex.

Besides the waste of money, the guilt made her irritable. Knowing her husband would be angry, she'd attack him first. A mood of defeat and wary hostility would settle over the whole family. When everyone calmed down, she'd come up with yet another plan to control herself: she'd shop only on weekends, or buy only on-sale items, or set a monthly spending limit. Needless to say, these plans always failed.

I told her that what she was missing was willpower. "Where can I buy that?" she asked, half-joking. I explained that it wasn't for sale, but if she was willing to do a little work, she could develop it for herself. She trained herself to use the Jeopardy tool every time she went near her computer. In the beginning, it didn't stop her from going online or even buying things, but the thrill was gone. "When I see that deathbed figure trying to save me from my own stupidity, I just can't lose myself like I used to." For the first time in her life, she was able to shop without compulsion.

Jeopardy gives you the strength to concentrate in circumstances where you usually space out or get distracted. *We've become a society of hyperactive multitaskers, with the attention span of a flea. We need a force strong enough to hold our concentration on one thing until we're finished with it. That takes willpower.*

Alex was an outgoing, high-energy Hollywood agent who had begun to lose clients. He was confused about this, because he was making good deals for them. I encouraged him to ask one of them why he'd left. The answer shocked him. The client said he didn't feel like he was important to Alex. When Alex pointed to the lucrative deal he'd gotten for the client, he answered, "It's not about money; you make me feel like a second-class citizen. You're always doing two other things when you're on the phone with me, you barely focus on what I'm saying."

Alex had never been able to concentrate. He had charmed his way through school and into a great career. But beneath the surface, he felt like his whole life had been a fake. He'd go into every meeting unprepared, rarely having read the script he was trying to sell. His marriage felt equally fraudulent. He was no longer close to his wife; on the rare occasion when he took her out he was either on the phone or talking to the people at the next table. He couldn't even focus on his chosen distractions. He needed a second cellphone to interrupt calls to his first.

He was a classic candidate for Jeopardy. If he couldn't learn to concentrate, everything he'd worked for was at risk. The cue I identified for him was simple: every time he felt the temptation to distract himself, he'd use Jeopardy to create the willpower to bring his focus back to where it belonged. I knew he'd have plenty of opportunities to practice. He was astounded at how weak his concentration really was. "I'm distracted every second. I could use breathing as a cue."

As difficult as using Jeopardy was, he stuck with it. For him, it was a milestone to be able to focus on a script for twenty minutes. As his concentration got better, there was a completely unexpected bonus. "I've spent my whole life dancing as fast as I could so I wouldn't be discovered. Now I walk into meetings having done my homework. I feel like a grown man for the first time."

Jeopardy enables you to start new ventures. *One of the hardest things to do in life is to start something new: moving to a new city, developing a relationship with someone thrust into your life (stepchildren, in-laws, etc.), starting a new business. Each of these steps—and any other new undertaking—triggers the most primal of human fears: fear of the unknown. We gravitate toward the familiar, even if it's not good for us, because we lack the will to push through that fear. Jeopardy creates a force of will stronger than our fear.*

Harriet was married to a much older man who had grown children from a prior marriage. He was the boss of a highly successful company that he'd built from scratch and reigned over his employees with absolute authority. Unfortunately, he knew no other way to relate to people. He provided for Harriet's material needs, but controlled every aspect of their lives. She had been willing to put up with this for years, denying how much it bothered her.

But she had one desire she couldn't deny; she wanted a child. She pled and argued—to no avail. Her husband wouldn't even discuss it with her. That was the breaking point. Finally, she knew in her heart she couldn't stay in the marriage. But years of living in a cocoon had left her completely helpless. Not only was the prospect of being on her own terrifying, she had no idea how to take even an initial step toward leaving the marriage. She needed to enter a world of lawyers, accountants, real-estate agents, etc. "My husband always dealt with those people. I thought of it as happening on another planet."

I told her that none of it was even remotely beyond her ability. Her terror was because the world she was entering represented the unknown. For Harriet, or anyone else, that's like stepping off the edge of a cliff. She needed a force that would allow her to act in the face of overwhelming fear. Jeopardy was the perfect tool. The moment she saw the reaction of her deathbed self to being childless, she experienced an electrifying urgency she'd never felt in her life. Not only was she able to dissolve the marriage, she continued using Jeopardy to construct a new life for herself.

What the Tool Is For

By now, you should know how to use each of the basic tools described in Chapters 2 through 5. But no matter how effective they've been, you'll find yourself quitting them. Not only will quitting stop your progress, it will destroy all the gains you've made up until this point. This is the fundamental obstacle every reader faces.

What You're Fighting Against

The illusion that you can obtain a "magical something" that will exonerate you from using the tools. This is reinforced day and night by the consumer culture that surrounds you. The illusion always leads to the same result: you quit. In success, you think the tools are no longer necessary; and in failure, you're too demoralized to use them.

Cues to Use the Tool

1. In any situation where you know you need a tool but, for whatever reason, can't get yourself to use one.
2. When you feel you've grown beyond the need for the tools.

The Tool in Brief

See yourself lying on your deathbed. Having run out of time, this older self screams at you not to waste the present moment. You feel a deep, hidden fear that you've been squandering your life. This creates an urgent desire to use whichever basic tool you need at that moment.

The Higher Force You're Using

You can't overcome the tendency to quit by thinking about it. You need a higher force. We call that force willpower. It's the one higher force you must create yourself; all the universe can do is provide a challenge that demands you generate it.

CHAPTER 7

Faith in Higher Forces

YOU'LL GET AN AMAZING WINDFALL WHEN YOU become a creator: you'll start to have faith that higher forces are there when you need them.

When I first met Phil, I didn't believe that higher forces were real, let alone that I could rely on them for support. As I learned the tools, I could tell that they worked—my patients were living proof. But as to *how* they worked, I didn't believe Phil when he said they evoked higher forces; I didn't even believe my patients when they attributed it to "something greater" than themselves. I figured that was their way of expressing how much better they felt.

As I explained in Chapter 1, my skepticism came naturally—I was raised with it. My parents were atheists: they believed in science, not God, and they would have scoffed at anything like "higher forces" that couldn't be explained logically. To them, the universe (and everything that happened in it) was nothing more than a random accident. In short, *faith* was my family's "f-word." I eagerly absorbed their belief system (rationalism), adopting it as my own. I occasionally paid a price for this socially; when I was nine years old, I had a sleepover with a friend who belonged to a religious family. When my friend's mother tucked us in, she noticed I wasn't praying and she asked me why. I naively took this as an opportunity to explain logically why God didn't exist. Needless to say, that was my last sleepover at my friend's house.

As the years passed, my views only hardened. As a consequence, although I appreciated the tools and used them effectively, I knew I was missing something. The tools gave me a better way to function and I was certainly grateful for that. But there were patients who experienced them in a way I was incapable of. When they used the tools in front of me, it was obvious they were connecting to something much bigger than themselves. Their faces radiated joy, contentment, and confidence at a level I'd never experienced. To me, the universe still seemed indifferent; to them, it had become a source of ever-present help. It felt like they had broken through the sound barrier while I was limping, with great effort, on the ground below them.

This created a strange set of feelings in me. If the tools were the course of study, my patients were getting higher marks than I was. This was one of the only times in my life I didn't come out at the top of the class. Frankly, it felt unfair. They weren't working any harder than I was; they just didn't have to contend with an inner skeptic who attacked the idea of higher forces at every turn. Yet, to my surprise, I could feel myself urging them on. Secretly, I hoped to be able to feel the way they did.

My inner skeptic had other ideas. He attacked the tool (Active Love) that could help me with my weakest area: resentment. It didn't matter what was happening in my life, I was always up in arms about something. I resented my kids when they woke me up at night, my wife for pushing me to accompany her to social events, my patients when they called me after hours, etc. As soon as one resentment faded, another took its place. I came to call it "resentment in search of a cause."

My inner skeptic couldn't stop me from using Active Love, and when I used the tool it helped, mostly by giving me something to do every time I felt resentful. But I never really felt a powerful love flowing through me. I knew it was there somewhere—I had felt it when my wife gave birth to each of my two children. But as deep as those feelings were, they weren't the same thing as being able to summon up a more universal love that I could direct at anyone. To do that, the tool required me to believe that I was surrounded by pure, cosmic love. But the inner skeptic had long ago convinced me that that was a romantic fantasy: I was living in a mechanical universe and love was just a product of brain chemistry. Skepticism had effectively drained the life out of the tool.

I fought back in the only way I knew how—with pure,

dogged persistence. I practiced the tool over and over again. I even set my watch to beep every hour as a cue to use the tool. I did this for months.

Just as I was about to lose hope, my efforts paid off in a way I never could've imagined.

January 17, 1993, was my son's first birthday. But before dawn, long before it was time to give him his gifts, I received a gift of my own—it was a dream I will never forget. In the dream, it was the early morning and I was alone in my office. Suddenly, the whole building began to shake violently. It was a massive earthquake and I knew that in seconds I was going to die. Uncharacteristically calm, I thought to myself, I should use Active Love one last time, so I can die with love in my heart. But this time when I used the tool, I was flooded with a love greater than any I'd ever felt. I felt the tremendous force of that love expanding me from the inside, as if the sun were radiating from my heart. Then the dream was over.

It was one of those dreams that stayed with me for weeks, resounding through my life. I felt more alive—the abundant love I'd felt in the dream continued to flow through me toward everyone, from the gas-station attendant to my wife and children. My patients felt it, commenting that I seemed even more enthusiastic than usual about their growth and that it was inspiring them to work harder on themselves.

I also began to look at the world differently. Everything around me seemed overflowing with life. I began to see more deeply into my patients' dynamics, and I was able to make connections for them that I'd never been able to make. I even began to wonder if certain events in my life had been planned out ahead of time by a higher intelligence. Was I propelled to quit law, not just because I hated it, but because I needed to open myself up to a whole new worldview? It no longer felt coincidental that I had met Phil right at the time I was disillusioned with the traditional approach to psychotherapy.

I'd studied Jung carefully, and I knew he didn't believe in coincidences. I appreciated the mystery and beauty of this view, but it had no more impact on my real life than a masterful painting hanging in a museum. The dream had changed this. Now, I could somehow feel a hidden connection between all the events in my life. This impression was so strong it even led me beyond Jung. It was as if the universe was guiding me in the direction of my own evolution.

My parents would have scoffed at such wild speculations, and it was deeply disturbing to find myself entertaining them. All of this love flowing through me certainly made it easier to use tools (it was like Active Love on steroids), but I also felt like I didn't quite know myself. Why was I suddenly feeling these things? I hoped Phil had an answer.

"Am I in some kind of an altered state?" I asked him. "It feels a little like temporary insanity."

"Absolutely not," he answered firmly. "You're saner than you've ever been."

"How can you call it sanity when I'm having all these crazy ideas?"

"Maybe the ideas aren't crazy," he suggested with a flash of irritation. "Maybe what's crazy would be returning to the way you were living before the dream."

He had a point. I felt really alive now. My former life seemed pale in comparison. "I wouldn't want to return to that," I answered slowly, "but you're asking me to change everything I believe just because of a dream."

Phil seemed disappointed for a moment. But then all tension drained from his body and he seemed to shut out everything except me. His eyes radiated understanding. It wasn't until later that I realized he was using Active Love. "I don't want to talk you into anything," he said. "Life will do that in its own way."

I left the conversation feeling I was on the edge of a mystery I didn't understand. But before I could make sense of it, all the new feelings faded. I found myself back in my familiar, mechanistic grind. If I thought about that period at all, it was with embarrassment; my rational mind, back in control, discounted the whole experience as a miniature midlife crisis—without the sports car. But secretly, I missed the sense of aliveness that the mystery had brought me; eventually, that went away, too. I even forgot the dream that had kick-started the whole thing.

That's when the unimaginable occurred.

On January 17, 1994, exactly one year to the day after the dream, the costliest earthquake in U.S. history struck

Los Angeles in the early hours before dawn. The building that housed my office collapsed. Everything in it was pulverized.

HUMPTY DUMPTY HAS A GREAT FALL

The earthquake destroyed my office, but that was the least of the damage. It also destroyed my belief system. To paraphrase Hamlet, it suddenly seemed that there were more things in heaven and earth than my philosophy had ever dreamed of. Here were the facts: two heart-opening events had occurred, the first on January 17, 1992, (the day my son was born) and the second on January 17, 1993, (when I had the earthquake dream). Now, on January 17, 1994, an actual earthquake had ripped through Los Angeles. My rational background would have led me to the smug conclusion that these events were purely coincidental. But now, rationalism felt like a toxic substance my body was rejecting. In fact, I suspected the earthquake would turn out to be as much of a gift as the first two events had.

Meanwhile, my life went on. I secured temporary office space and worked to bring some sense of normality back to my practice. But I couldn't let go of the idea that the last few years of my life had been guided by some cosmic intelligence. It had pushed me to quit law, gotten me to become a psychotherapist, and arranged for me to meet Phil. Then, it entered my life more directly, choreographing the birth of my son and a life-changing dream exactly a year apart.

But those events were subtle compared to what had happened now. It was as if this higher intelligence—determined to drive a stake through my rationalism—had anticipated a major disaster and used it as the final weapon.

It had worked. I could never rely on rationalism again. But as I considered the alternatives, it was clear they were even worse. On the one hand, there was organized religion, which had always struck me as dogmatic and authoritarian. As a Jew, I'd always wondered why I should accept the commandment never to mix meat and milk (as I wondered about equally inexplicable customs in other religions). The answer always seemed to come down to "you should believe these things because we tell you to" (or because "it is written"). These responses seemed to imply that I wasn't supposed to think for myself.

On the other hand, there was the New Age mysticism that, in Southern California, was as ubiquitous as movie-star sightings. It certainly allowed for free thinking and offered plenty of experiences (real or not). But it was also as unrelentingly sunny and without substance as Los Angeles, the city that spawned it. Visualize what you want to be doing in five years, and presto—it will happen! Every problem could be solved by happy talk. But what if there were painful, even horrible problems that couldn't be solved? New Age philosophy had no answer except to blame the sufferer. "Your negative thoughts gave you cancer," one patient of mine was told by her New Age friends. Something had to be missing from a philosophy that found no meaning or purpose in adversity; and if it couldn't handle everyday adversity, how could it possibly deal with true evil—like the pogroms and death camps that had killed so many of my relatives.

I was at a dead end. I loved my new life as a psychotherapist—the ability to have a positive impact on people's lives was personally more fulfilling than anything I'd ever done. But this was about more than my personal fulfillment; it seemed to be about the nature of reality. My rationalism looked like a squashed bug, a part of my past I'd left in the rearview mirror. The problem was that I couldn't move forward. The two paths I saw in front of me were unacceptable.

When all the king's horses and all the king's men can't put you back together again, the universal human reaction is . . . dread. For weeks, I felt like my heart was pounding out of my chest. Only because I didn't know what else to do, I turned to Phil. But this time I didn't approach him as an enthusiastic student; I came as a drowning man.

"Do you feel like everything you've ever believed was wrong?" he asked.

I nodded.

"Congratulations," he said warmly. "You've been introduced to the spirituality of the future."

Weirdly, this made sense to me. What he meant was that new ideas cannot enter until old, rigid ones are shattered. This affirmed what I'd intuited about the earthquake, that it was the climax in a sequence of events designed to sweep aside my old belief system.

But what would I replace it with? Suspicious and hopeful at the same time, I demanded he explain this "new spirituality" on the spot. This was completely out of character for me, but I couldn't help it: I had the feeling this was going to be a life-changing conversation. I turned out to be right.

Phil explained that there exists a "spiritual system" that connects every human being to the universe. Logical objections lit up my mind like a pinball machine, but before I could say anything, Phil whipped out a three-by-five-inch index card and began to draw a strange picture—all the while continuing to talk. What he said distracted me from my doubts and I kept my mouth shut.

We've all been taught physical evolution, Phil said. In this model, evolution is driven by random genetic changes that give us a better chance of survival. The universe has no particular goal for us; in fact, it doesn't even know we exist. This model does a good job of explaining *physical* evolution. But there's another kind of evolution—best called "spiritual evolution"—that has to do with the development of the inner self. The inner self can evolve only by choosing to gain access to higher forces.

I began to object and was interrupted by a sharp crack—like somebody had fired a pistol. I jumped, but it was the sound of Phil slapping the index card on the desk like a gambler who's drawn an inside straight.

"See this? Inner evolution is driven by this system," he said, referring to the picture on the card. "Just get inside the system. When you're in there, you'll experience something so strong it'll wash away your doubts."

This did not satisfy my skepticism. Nothing was going to wash that away. But Phil saw the arguments forming in my mind and declared abruptly, "No more debate. Study the card and get inside the system. If you still need an explanation, we'll talk later."

There was no arguing with him. He was adamant. My task was simple: participate in the system and experience what he called "higher forces." It was all spelled out in the following diagram:

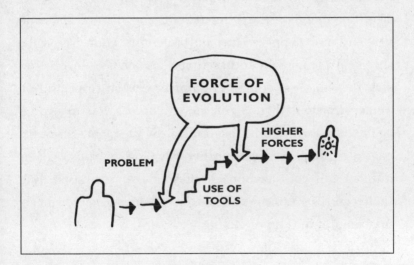

The figure on the left is faced with a life problem; it might be an illness, a job loss, or even the inner confusion I was going through. As the first thick arrow indicates, the problem is sent down by the force that governs evolution (which you can call God, Higher Power, etc.). Then the person uses tools to resolve the problem, illustrated by the steps. They lead upward to an expanded level of existence where he has access to higher forces, allowing him to do things he's never done before. This reveals the hidden purpose of the entire spiritual system: to enable us to become creators. In the picture, creatorship is represented by the sun inside the figure on the far right.

The drawing reveals an amazing secret: both the problem and the higher forces that solve it come from the same source—the Force of Evolution. These two elements are part of one system, designed to transform you into a creator. But there's a third ingredient, and it's one the universe cannot supply. That ingredient is your free will; specifically, your will to use tools. The choice—evolve or stay the same—is yours. The universe is so respectful of human freedom that it refuses to compel you to evolve against your will. (In fact, if you review the rabbi's story on page 206, you'll see that the only way God's purpose can be fulfilled is if you take charge of your own evolution. But that requires a strong will, which is why we made such a fuss about it in Chapter 6.)

HOW I LEARNED TO LOVE EGGS

All of this sounded great, but none of it silenced the objections screaming in my head. I tried to voice them but Phil would listen only for so long. He wanted me to *work inside the system*, not debate its validity, so he ordered me to identify a problem, choose a tool and (his words), "shut up and use the tool" every time I experienced the problem.

At the time, the problem I identified had to do with my best friend, Steve. Secretly I'd always felt insecure around him. I was smart, but he was beyond smart. He excelled at everything—from gymnastics to the history of Afghanistan. When we were fourteen years old, he mesmerized a crowd of adult theatergoers at the intermission of *King Richard III* with an impromptu lecture on Tudor England and Shakespeare's motivation for turning the king into a despicable hunchback.

While I was raised by parents who *believed* in science, he was raised by parents who *were* scientists. He himself became a world-class theoretical physicist. Steve dismissed anything that wasn't explainable in terms of observable, physical phenomena. When I said I could feel Jimi Hendrix's soul coming through his guitar, he corrected me, explaining that all sound—including music—was nothing more than "mechanical vibrations transmitted through the air."

We loved each other like brothers, but the more I absorbed these new, spiritual ideas, the more afraid I was that, if I dared voice them, he'd incisively destroy them. So when he called and said he wanted to have lunch to find out more about my work, I had a completely inappropriate reaction. I found myself in an endless loop of imaginary arguments with him about science versus spirituality. Steve was a brilliant, daunting adversary who—in my mind—crushed me every time. I completely lost sight of the real brotherhood between us; the more I obsessed, the more I resented him.

I knew my reaction was ridiculous; I hated myself for turning my best friend into a threatening rival. But nothing helped. No matter how many patients I'd seen go through this, I was lost in the Maze and I couldn't find a way out.

I explained my worst fear to Phil: "I'm going to feel like a complete idiot."

"Steve may be brilliant, but he's only human," Phil replied reasonably.

But Phil had never met Steve. "You don't understand. He invalidated Hendrix's soul in one sentence; imagine what he'll do to higher forces."

"That's not important," Phil said blithely. "The important thing is to experience what's happening as part of the spiritual system." To make the whole thing idiotproof, he showed me the diagram again. The "problem" was my Maze-like obsession with the upcoming lunch. The tool would be Active Love, which I would use whenever I felt resentment toward Steve.

I practiced the tool as he told me to, but I still felt like an amateur lightweight preparing to challenge the heavyweight champion of the world. More obsessed than ever, I went back to Phil and complained, "I don't think this is going to work."

"What you think doesn't matter," Phil barked. "Focus on what you do, not on what you think. Your only job is to use the tool. The system will do the rest." As he swept me out the door, I imagined him chanting, Problem—tool; problem—tool.

I was baffled and demoralized . . . but I had no options. So I used Active Love doggedly, every time my thoughts veered toward the lunch. Gradually, I began to notice myself feeling different. I was a little less afraid of Steve's judgment and more excited about expressing myself.

Before I knew it, the day came. I used Active Love on my way to the restaurant and then a few more times when I saw Steve sitting at a table. After we greeted each other and ordered, I could see that the moment of truth had arrived. Steve looked straight at me and said professorially, "So how would you describe your orientation to psychotherapy?"

When I heard his tone I felt my old anxiety coming up again. I used Active Love. "I . . . I guess I have a 'spiritual' orientation."

"That's interesting. What's that?"

I closed my eyes and took a deep breath. When I started to speak, what came out amazed me. "What if every bad thing that's ever happened to you—including every problem you've ever had—was there, in your life, to get you in touch with abilities you never knew you had? And what if there were specific procedures that led you directly to those new abilities?"

I saw his eyes light up.

Carried by a wave of passion, I launched into an explanation of the spiritual system Phil had described. But I was no longer spouting Phil's words; the system had become a part of me. In my natural excitement, I completely forgot that these ideas were improvable and that I was talking to a scientist. I no longer felt like a rival, like I had to defend the ideas or defeat Steve. All I felt was inspired.

When I was finished, I looked at Steve. He was beaming (maybe it was just me, but he'd lost his professorial demeanor). "This is great, Barry! You've found something you really believe in, and I bet you've helped a lot of people with it."

I was stunned. "You mean you accept the premises . . . the spiritual system and everything?"

"In a strict sense, no." He shrugged his shoulders. "But you know what Pascal said: 'It's the heart that feels God, not the reasoning powers.'"

I couldn't believe what I was hearing. "What are you saying?"

He took a deep breath. "You get results. Sometimes that's all that matters."

I still didn't understand. He thought for a while, then suddenly grinned. "This old joke explains it better. A guy goes to see his psychiatrist. He says, 'Doc, my brother's crazy, he thinks he's a chicken. What should I do?' The shrink answers, 'You'll need to hospitalize him.' And the man says, 'I can't. . . . I need the eggs.'"

After I stopped laughing I realized Steve had just said it better than I ever could have. He was telling me that the spiritual system produced "eggs" for the patients and it didn't matter how they were helped.

That lunch was a turning point for me. I now saw that Steve wasn't the only person who put me in the Maze; most people did. I'd been laboring under the false assumption that, if I tried to express myself in a way that the other person disagreed with, he or she would shut me down. Little wonder I walked around with so much resentment; I felt silenced by everyone around me—when in fact I was stifling myself! It was like being in a prison cell and discovering I'd had the key in my pocket the whole time—and the key was Active Love.

I began to use the tool with everyone—friends, patients, family—and my resentments seemed to evaporate. I was amazed at how much better I felt. Now I noticed myself looking people in the eye, speaking directly to them, feeling more relaxed and confident. Whether they agreed or disagreed with me became irrelevant. I could also feel real love flowing through me, just as I could after the dream. Only this time, it didn't go away; my heart remained open, and I felt more alive.

Just as Phil had predicted, my doubts were gone. I had experienced higher forces moving in my life, changing me for the better. I couldn't prove the existence of higher forces logically, but I no longer felt the need to. I began to understand what faith really meant: *faith is the confidence that higher forces are always there to help when you need them.*

Clearly, what I had gone through was profound. I

couldn't help but look at Phil differently after it was over. I had always thought of him as a bit fanatical. But he had never tried to shove his ideas down my throat—he didn't try to influence me at all. At my darkest moment, he showed absolute faith that a spiritual system was at work, teaching me what I needed to learn. If he wasn't a fanatic, where did this faith come from? I decided, as usual, to ask him directly. We had an unforgettable conversation.

When Barry asked me directly where my faith came from, it marked a turning point in our relationship. My patients never asked me that question, it was too personal. I could tell what they were thinking. Whenever I expressed confidence in the spiritual system, they looked at me as if I were a well-meaning eccentric. Later, after they reaped the benefits of that system, they looked at me as if I were some kind of clairvoyant genius.

Both looks missed the point. I am just a human being who has learned to trust what life brings me. I admit that my life has been a bit unusual. All through school and psychiatric training, I was bursting with energy and enthusiasm. Then things took an unexpected turn. As I was beginning my psychiatric practice, I started to get tired—not the everyday fatigue that comes from overwork. This was a bone-deep exhaustion far beyond anything I'd ever felt.

The exhaustion crept up like a thief in the night. At first, I'd feel all right during the week; but when the weekend came, I'd collapse and sleep until Monday. Then, one Monday morning, I woke up and the thief was still there. I could barely get out of bed. I took off a week from work—the first time I'd ever done that in my life—but at the end of the week, I felt even more exhausted. Something had to give; I tried to buy off the thief by giving up exercise and my social life. But that wasn't enough.

The only thing I was allowed to do was to continue my practice—albeit at a much lower level of energy. Life now consisted of seeing patients and then going back to bed. For months, I told myself this was only temporary. Finally, when things hadn't improved at all, I began to wonder if I'd ever recover.

With some hesitation, I dragged myself to an internist. I went to an old medical-school classmate of mine who was an excellent physician and all-around nice guy. He was all ears when I told him the story. When it was over, he told me what tests he'd run and what some of the possibilities were. Every single test—and there were a slew of them—was normal. He suggested we redo them a few weeks later. We did and the tests were still normal, but I was even worse. After that, there was a subtle change in his manner. It wasn't an I'm-glad-to-see-you smile. It was the kind of smile you gave someone on the subway who you suspect just walked out of Bellevue.

I was about to become very familiar with that smile. I saw it on the faces of an untold number of specialists I went to, trying to track down what was robbing me of my life force. It didn't bother me that they had no idea what was going on. What bugged me was their conclusion. Since they couldn't explain it, in their minds it must not be happening at all; which meant they thought I was some kind of a madman.

After I don't know how many consultations, I decided I would seek help only from those who believed something was actually happening. I quickly found out that there was only one person who fit that description: me.

Looking back, that was the first hint that the illness had a purpose. It had already shut me off from most of the outside world, I spent almost no time outside my office or my bed. But the realization that there was no one out there who could help me felt like another door had closed. Make that two doors; this was also the time period when I lost confidence in the therapeutic model I'd been taught. There was nobody out there to help me with that, either.

I didn't realize it at the time, but this loss of connection to the outside world was the most important thing that had ever happened to me. Life was forcing me to enter an inner world I never would have chosen on my own. At first, I resented losing my connection to the world outside. I felt like life had passed me by. But before long, I realized the inner world was the real source of life.

Besides seeing patients, my other activity was sleeping. . . . I should say, trying to sleep. Sometimes I'd toss and turn for twelve hours. I had no fever, but I'd feel a strange heat, almost like I was being liquefied. This happened every night. Something was relentlessly trying to reach me from the inner world.

And it did. The evidence came in the sessions with my patients. As I struggled to create the tools they needed, the information I needed seemed to appear from nowhere. It certainly wasn't coming from anyone in the outside world, nor was I figuring it out in my head. Answers that I didn't know I knew were coming out of my mouth, as if I were a spokesperson for some other force. I couldn't prove it, but I could feel it.

So could the patients—even the most resistant ones—once they started using the tools. These were ones who had been rejecting every interpretation I gave. Working with them was like carving marble with a plastic spoon. But once I began to give them tools, everything shifted. The change agent was no longer me; it was the higher forces they evoked with the tools. It was humbling and inspiring at the same time.

As debilitating as the illness was, it led me to what I needed, access to the inner world and tools to evoke the higher forces buried there. It began to dawn on me that my patients and I were functioning within a spiritual system. In it, every event in our lives was designed to train us in the use of higher forces. My "event" was a chronic illness with no apparent cause or cure.

For me, this system was far from theoretical. I was a living graduate of its training program. Barry had asked me how I knew that life would teach him what he needed to learn. The effects of my illness gave me the answer. I now knew that we live in a deeply caring universe that has a purpose for each of us. I had felt its love working in my own life in a way I couldn't have imagined. How could such a universe *not* teach us what we needed to learn?

That was the answer to Barry's question.

When Phil was finished, I felt as though the breath had been taken out of me. I hadn't expected to hear something so personal. The spiritual system wasn't just a concept he'd discovered, he'd really lived in it—and found positive meaning in his suffering. I'd never felt closer to him. He'd gone to medical school and I'd gone to law school, but we'd learned faith from the same teacher: life.

CHAPTER 8

The Fruits of a New Vision

THE FAITH WE LEARNED FROM LIFE WASN'T A "blind faith." It was based on patterns we could actually see in the spiritual world. Phil and I spent a long time trying to understand those patterns, and we were finally able to describe them in a way that anyone could understand. What we observed formed the pillars of a new spirituality.

Once we identified them, we were gratified (and a little amazed) to find many ways in which modern consciousness was already reflecting this new spiritual order. Higher forces had been entering the world; they were changing the way we operated as a society.

Pillar 1: Thinking about higher forces is worthless, you have to experience them.

As modern people, we don't realize the degree to which our perception is limited by the scientific model. Science accepts nothing that can't be proven logically. That's what led me, in Chapter 7, to demand that Phil prove that higher forces were real. He had no interest in doing that; he knew higher forces existed in a realm not subject to the scientific model. It's an inner world you must enter; it can't be understood with thinking—that's just inside your head. In the inner world, what's real is what affects your whole being. By insisting that I use a tool to solve my problem, Phil was guiding me to enter the inner world and experience the higher forces that exist there.

He was demonstrating the first pillar of the new spirituality: You can't prove or disprove the existence of higher forces; *they're only real for you if you can feel them.*

The philosopher Kierkegaard hinted at this principle when he wrote, "Life has its own hidden forces which you can only discover by living." Say you're a war refugee who's lost contact with your family; imagine the difference between getting a document that notifies you that they're alive versus the life-altering experience of actually reuniting with them. That's the difference between knowing something in your head and experiencing it with your whole being. Only your whole being can experience higher forces as real.

This is a radically new way of evaluating what's real. We've been trained to do that through thinking, but that doesn't work with higher forces. The moment you start to think, you're in your head, demanding proof that they exist. Higher forces must be *experienced directly*, and that takes effort. That means you'll face the same stark choice I did: demand proof that you'll never receive, or use the tools in the face of your doubts. When I stopped thinking and focused on the tools, my reward was life-changing faith. I hope you make the same choice.

This new way of perceiving reality has already crept into society. Everyone has some knowledge of Alcoholics Anonymous and the greater Twelve Step movement. True to the first pillar of the new spirituality, AA elevates experience over belief. I've seen alcoholics enter AA disagreeing with everything about it—yet the program saved their lives. The program bypasses what you think; if you work the steps, you begin to experience forces greater than yourself helping you stay sober.

Even modern scientists occasionally concede the presence of a realm beyond the reach of scientific proof. A famous story about Niels Bohr, the great Danish physicist and father of quantum theory, exemplifies this. A young physicist visited him in his home and saw a horseshoe hanging on the wall over the hearth. "Surely, professor, you don't believe that a horseshoe will bring you good luck," the young physicist exclaimed. "Of course not!" Bohr replied. "But I've heard that you don't have to believe in it for it to work."

Pillar 2: When it comes to spiritual reality, each of us is his own authority.

Until you can experience spiritual forces with your whole being, you're stuck in the same trap I was in: you can either accept what spiritual authority figures tell you to believe, or reject it (as I did). Either way, you aren't experiencing higher forces for yourself, so you can't come to any intelligent conclusions about them. That leads us to the second pillar: *in the new spirituality, each individual must experience higher forces and arrive at his own conclusions about their nature; external authority figures can no longer define our spiritual reality for us.*

This takes us beyond what we normally think of as traditional religion. In ancient times, an authority figure (a priest or the like) would interpret the divine on behalf of an entire community. The word of these religious leaders was universally accepted as the Word of God. To varying degrees, organized religion still subscribes to this old "top-down" hierarchy. Organized around a leader, most congregations defer to his superior understanding of the divine. This doesn't respect the modern person's need to arrive at his own understanding.

That's where the new spirituality comes in. It is predicated on the fact that every human being is unique. It gives you tools and a methodology that allow you to explore higher forces so that you can experience their nature in your own way.

This was very important to me personally. As a young man I'd been trained to "Question Authority," as the old bumper sticker read. This was one of the reasons I'd rejected organized religion. Now, amazingly, Phil's approach *demanded* I question authority—even himself. He never tried to get me to agree with him; all he wanted was for me to use the tools and come to my own conclusions.

As it turns out, I'm no longer alone in wanting to forge my own path. Increasingly, an entire cohort of people want to decide things for themselves. Although the United States is one of the most religious countries in the world, the views of most Americans don't fit neatly into one religion; often they contradict the teachings of their own faith. There are Catholics who meditate and Protestants who pray to the Virgin Mary (not to mention the number of Jewish Buddhists). It's condescending to think people do this out of ignorance—in increasing numbers, people want to choose what works for them based on their own spiritual instincts.

Once again Alcoholics Anonymous is a good example of this. It wasn't developed from the top down, by medical experts, but from the bottom up (no pun intended), by alcoholics. Its founder, Bill Wilson, wasn't a doctor; he was a stock speculator. His authority came from the fact that he couldn't get through a day without passing out from alcohol. People fighting addiction every day turned out to be the most qualified to know what helps. They concluded that only a Higher Power was strong enough to overcome addiction.

Pillar 3: Personal problems drive the evolution of the individual.

Without my insecurity around my friend Steve, I never would've achieved the confidence I feel today. Without a crippling illness, Phil never would've taken the inner journey that yielded the tools. These are illustrations of the third pillar of the new spirituality: *the driving force of spiritual evolution is personal problems.*

This principle makes sense to people in the abstract, but when you're facing heavy adversity—a foreclosure, loss of a job, or the death of a loved one—most people find it hard to see the upside. The following exercise can help. It's a way of putting yourself right inside the system depicted in Phil's drawing. Think of a particularly difficult problem you have in your life right now and then try this:

> First, think of the problem as a random hardship, occurring in an unthinking universe that doesn't care about you or your evolution. How does that feel? Now, think of the same problem as a challenge posed by a universe that wants you to evolve and knows that you can. How does that feel?

Most people feel more motivated when they envision themselves as part of an intelligent system whose goal is their advancement. After my lunch with Steve, I made it a point to think of all my problems this way. The results were immediate: I was eager to work on my problems because I felt they were there for my benefit.

This ongoing sense that problems are meaningful is a fundamental difference between a consumer and a creator. A consumer feels that life is only meaningful when his needs are being gratified. Problems, because they are ungratifying, inevitably destroy the consumer's sense of purpose. In contrast, a creator has a sense of meaning that can't be destroyed—he insists on seeing problems as driving him toward something better, something higher in himself. Far from destroying his sense of meaning, problems actually reinforce it.

Our entire society seems ready to see problems in this new way. That's why we're more interested than we've ever been in problems. For many, it's too painful to face their own problems so they become obsessed with the problems of celebrities. No matter what country you're in, you can find people fascinated with a politician caught in a love triangle, a sports idol who assaulted his girlfriend, or an actress who failed her latest drug test. We need to become as focused on our own problems as we are on those of celebrities.

Certainly the desire is there. It's revealed in the astronomical growth in the use of psychotherapy since Freud introduced psychoanalysis in the early 1900s. The explanation for this increase is simple: therapy is the place we go to solve our problems. It's easy to disparage the rise of psychotherapy as a symptom of our self-absorption—millions of Woody Allens running amok in society. But we've found that even the most self-absorbed patient on some level senses the crucial importance of problems in driving their evolution.

But until very recently, psychotherapy has focused more on the causes of problems than on the solutions. Sixty years ago, it was acceptable, in a course of psychoanalysis, to talk about your problems five days a week while doing nothing to solve them. Today, the average patient wants more. They want to develop hidden capacities, and they're willing to do the work to make that happen.

They want to respond to their problems as creators. All they need are the right tools.

When psychotherapy acknowledges this need, it will revolutionize the profession. In fact, it's the ultimate irony: psychotherapy, the brainchild of Sigmund Freud (a confirmed atheist), will become a spiritual endeavor.

Clearly, God has a sense of humor.

I've seen the growing acceptance of spirituality in my own practice. There's a certain type of psychotherapy patient—well educated, hip, ironic, with little or no religious background (usually dressed all in black)—who would have sneered at the notion of higher forces twenty or thirty years ago. Now, working with this same type, I find myself describing spiritual solutions in the first session and they embrace it. Sometimes they surprise me with statements such as "I believe everything happens for a reason." These people never intended to become spiritually open; they got swept up by an evolutionary wave that's affecting everyone's mind-set. If the wave has reached them, it's everywhere.

But evolution can carry us only so far without our active participation. To fulfill our evolutionary potential, the human race needs to take conscious responsibility for bringing higher forces into the world. As badly as the individual needs higher forces, the society at large needs them even more. Everything we cherish most hangs in the balance. The new spirituality is arriving just in time.

HEALING A SICK SOCIETY

Just as every individual has a spirit, so does society. Imagine the spirit of society as an organism, invisible but alive and weaving through all of us. The spirit is pure movement. It allows a society to embrace the future while at the same time creating harmony and understanding among its members.

If the spirit of a society is healthy, it's not afraid of change; it welcomes the new and can innovate in the face of challenges. Such a society pursues its aspirations confidently; it has faith in its future. Additionally, a strong spirit makes each person feel that they are part of a social organism—they feel responsible for the collective good and will sacrifice their individual interests for it.

But the spirit of our society isn't healthy. We've lost faith in our future; people are wary, closed off to new ideas, unwilling to take risks, even to spend or lend money. We've also lost faith in community—and with it the sense that we're all connected. It's every man for himself, with no one taking responsibility for the society at large.

When no one takes responsibility for anything but his or her own well-being, a civilization rots from within and finally collapses. The most famous example of this was the fall of the Roman Empire. Here's how Lewis Mumford, the eminent American historian, described it:

> *Everyone aimed at security; no one accepted responsibility. What was plainly lacking, long before the barbarian invasions . . . long before economic dislocations . . . was an inner go. Rome's life was now an imitation of life. . . . Security was the watchword—as if life knew any other stability than through constant change, or any form of security except through a constant willingness to take risks.*

What Mumford called the "inner go" corresponds exactly to what we're defining as the spirit of society. It's the moving force that gives life to a society and allows it to pursue its future with courage.

Our spirit used to be strong—strong enough to respond to World War II even after ten bitter years of economic hardship. Its strength came from the commitment of those we call the "Greatest Generation." And rightly so. Their greatness lay in the fact that they were willing to make enormous personal sacrifices for the sake of a higher good.

We are just as capable of greatness as they were. But we can't depend on a world war—or any outer event—to bring out our strength. As we've explained, evolution now requires that we give the best of ourselves, not because an outer event *compels* us to do so, but because we *choose to do so of our own free will.*

Free will must start with the individual. But can the spiritual vitality of one person affect the rest of society? It can; not only that, *it's the only thing that can.* Higher forces have always been, and still are, essential for successful societies. But in the past, they came through institutions, spiritual leaders, or sacred ceremonies and rituals; traditional channels that didn't involve ordinary individuals. Evolution now demands that higher forces enter society only through the individual. That's why those traditional channels—through corruption, paralysis, or irrelevance—are losing their influence. Until individuals are empowered to replace them, we are a society lacking faith and purpose.

Empowering individuals requires a revolution, but revolutions have always been fought against oppressors outside ourselves. Now, the enemy is inside, using each person's belief system against him. It uses science to convince some of us that higher forces don't exist—that no help is available. For others, it grants that higher forces exist, but insists that, to connect to them, we must stop thinking for ourselves and accept the views of some external authority figure.

In order to defeat the inner enemy, we need weapons that enable us to believe in and experience higher forces without sacrificing our freedom. You've already used them for your own benefit, without realizing their power to affect all of society. These weapons are the tools in this book.

Every time you use a tool and bring higher forces to bear on your own problems, you're also making them available to the society at large. Once you accept this, your problems become more than a source of self-absorption. They lead you beyond yourself to a concern for all of humanity. The tools make you a participant in a silent revolution—a revolution of creators. Only a creator can meet the evolutionary demand to change society while he changes himself.

How would it feel to be part of this revolution? You're about to find out. In the next five sections, you'll be using each tool to bring higher forces to bear on a personal problem. As you do this, we'll show you how to experience the effect these forces can have on the greater society.

WEAPONS FOR A SILENT REVOLUTION

Reversal of Desire

A healthy spirit has the confidence that it can meet the future. Although it's impossible to know exactly what the future will bring, it will definitely contain some type of pain. In our case, the "pain" will almost certainly take the form of economic (and possibly physical) threats to our well-being, difficult choices, as well as collective sacrifices. No society can achieve its aspirations unless it's willing to face these types of adversity.

This ability to face pain depends on the Force of Forward Motion. We talked about it in Chapter 2. It's the force that enables an individual life to expand and fulfill its potential because it is undaunted by pain. The ability to move forward into the future is just as important to a society.

When an individual stops moving forward in life, he stagnates. The same thing happens to a society. Its members stop facing reality and enter a collective Comfort Zone, indulging in the fantasy of getting what they want without having to sacrifice for it. For example, a consumer society mortgages its future to acquire things it can't afford.

When the Force of Forward Motion is missing, society loses its way. Instead of having real aspirations, we are left with empty, meaningless slogans, and our ideals die.

Our leaders don't help. They want us to believe we don't have to face reality—it makes their job easier. So they lie to us. But before you blame them, remember that they are a reflection of us: they can't tolerate pain, either. We can't expect them to embrace the pain of confronting the truth until we prove that we're willing to grapple with the truth ourselves.

Chapter 2 taught you the tool for facing pain. It's called

the Reversal of Desire. When you use it, it triggers a powerful force which overcomes your normal aversion to pain and propels you toward it. That force makes you unstoppable. When you use the tool and put yourself in motion, it affects more than just your own life. Because most human beings never leave their Comfort Zone, those who do have a profound impact on everybody else. Once you're in motion, you'll begin to see its effect on others around you. When they see and feel you doing things you've never done before, it expands their sense of what's possible for them. This is how the spirit of society is transformed.

Let's imagine what this might look like:

> Close your eyes and use the Reversal of Desire on
> something you normally avoid. Feel yourself starting
> to move forward. Now see those around you,
> inspired by your forward motion, using the tool on
> whatever they're avoiding. See millions of people
> embracing pain and as a result, moving forward in
> their lives. How does the society you're imagining
> look different from the one we have now?

When millions of individuals stop avoiding and start moving forward, there are no social problems they cannot solve. It's only a society that embraces pain that will lead the way for the rest of the world.

Active Love

A healthy spirit maintains a positive view of the future and constantly works to create that future. This requires an openness to new ideas, new ways of solving problems. When conditions are such that new ideas can't get a fair hearing, the spirit of society wanes.

In Chapter 3, we presented the concept of the Maze. As an individual, you get trapped in the Maze when you feel unfairly treated by someone and can't let go of it. All you can think about is what needs to happen to make you feel whole again. It's as if the other person has moved into your mind and taken up residence. While you're obsessing, life passes you by.

It's bad enough when this happens to an individual, but it's a disaster when a whole society falls into a collective Maze. The mind of that society closes. Instead of being a birthplace of new ideas, it becomes a crumbling monument to old ones. At that point, its spirit dies.

If you listen carefully to the public discussion in our society, you'll realize that new ideas aren't even being considered. Repetition is the hallmark of the Maze; it shuts out anything new. Just as the Maze traps an individual in the past, it can do that to an entire society. It's happening to us right now. Life is passing our society by while we continue the same debates we've had for decades.

The collective Maze reveals itself in the tone of our public discussion. It's strident, self-righteous, and contemptuous of anyone who dares to disagree. Almost by reflex, we make harsh judgments about all ideas that contradict our own. Our "national debate" has become a war in which nothing matters except winning. It feels like a fight to the death.

There's only one way to turn this situation around. It will sound radical, but we need to teach ourselves to accept all ideas, including the ones that offend us the most. We can't do this with our intellect. Only something greater than ourselves is powerful enough to create that level of acceptance. In Chapter 3, we called this higher force Outflow.

Outflow is generated through the human heart. On a cosmic level, the basic quality of the universe is Outflow. As human beings, we're blessed with the ability to create our own miniature version of it. When we do, something special happens. We sync up with cosmic Outflow. We're in harmony with a force infinitely larger than ourselves. At that moment, we have no need to judge any ideas, even ones we disagree with. Our security comes from a higher place.

Whether we realize it or not, Outflow underlies every public forum that is constructive. Without it, discussion becomes war. We lose hope that we can ever solve our problems.

Active Love is what makes it possible to generate Outflow, which frees the individual from the Maze. Let's take a look at what would happen collectively if enough people used the tool:

> Close your eyes and imagine someone whose ideas
> offend you deeply. Use Active Love on that person.
> Now use it again, but this time imagine the whole
> society using the tool on someone who offends
> them. How does society change with millions of
> people channeling this all-accepting force?

There is nothing more inspiring than to see a human being who is able to generate Outflow in the face of the worst judgment of all: vicious hatred. Martin Luther King, Jr., is an American icon for this reason—he employed Active Love (without calling it that) in order to prevent himself from falling into the Maze. He ended his sermon "Loving Your Enemies" this way: "So this morning, as I look into your eyes, and into the eyes of all of my brothers in Alabama and all over America and over the world, I say to you, 'I love you. I would rather die than hate you.' And I'm foolish enough to believe that through the power of this love somewhere, men of the most recalcitrant bent will be transformed."

Include the Shadow

Just as a strong spirit accepts new ideas, it also accepts all types of people. It sees the common humanity in everyone and therefore isn't threatened by different customs, beliefs, or ways of life. The strong spirit is interested in everyone and acts to include them.

In contrast, when the spirit is weak, we lose the common thread that connects us all. Without this thread, those who look, speak, and act differently from ourselves become the "other"—we fear them, look down on them, or blame them for our problems. No matter how tolerant you are, if you're honest with yourself you'll admit that there are people you regard as other. It might be a badly wounded veteran, a panhandling bum, or an entire ethnic group.

Behind the rejection of the other is a deeper rejection of a part of yourself. In Chapter 4 we introduced you to the Shadow: it's a separate being living inside of you. All the feelings you have for the other stem from your feelings toward this hidden part of yourself. Until you can accept this part of yourself, there is no accepting the other. Just as each of us is divided against himself, the greater society is divided against itself. *A society that cannot include the other is a society that has broken its own spirit.*

The only way to rebuild the spirit is to be true to its nature. The spirit always moves toward wholeness—it wants to embrace everyone. We feed the spirit every time we accept those who are most different from us. Doing this is a matter of self-interest. It's impossible for anyone to feel secure in a society at odds with itself. John Donne, the English poet, wrote, "No man is an island. . . . / any man's death diminishes me, / because I am involved with mankind. / And therefore never send to know for whom / the bell tolls; it tolls for thee."

The solution to the outer divisions in society has to

start inside of each individual. When you accept your Shadow, you discover that it's a source of higher forces. This will give those around you the courage to make the same discovery. The potency each individual gains from accepting the Shadow is a miniature model of the potential we can realize as a society that's been made whole.

This is how the spirit of a society revitalizes itself, one individual at a time. Here's what you, as an individual, need to do to start the process:

> Close your eyes and visualize your Shadow. Feel how embarrassed you would be if it were revealed to other people. Imagine millions of people around you feeling the same way about their Shadows, doing everything they can to conceal them. What happens to a society in which everyone's hearts are closed off to one another?
>
> Now, tell your Shadow you've been horribly mistaken, that you cannot be whole without it. Imagine millions of people saying the same thing to their Shadows. What can this open-hearted society do that the earlier one couldn't?

In Chapter 4, we used the Shadow as part of a tool called Inner Authority. When you accept your Shadow and become whole, you possess the ability to express yourself freely, which is actually very relevant to healing the spirit of our society. Everyone has a Shadow and every Shadow speaks a "language of the heart." Because this language is common to all of humanity, everyone feels included; no one is left out.

Grateful Flow

The spirit of a society depends on the support of all its members. Of particular importance are people in positions of authority. In a sense, they are the "stewards" of society, protecting its resources and exemplifying its ideals; they act as guardians of its spirit.

One of the reasons our society is so sick is that its stewards have failed to act in its best interests. They don't feel answerable to anything beyond themselves. In banking, law, medicine, politics, academia, and business, we've repeatedly seen individuals of power and privilege fail to safeguard the society at large. They've adopted an every-man-for-himself attitude.

The reason for this is hiding in plain sight. Almost everyone in our society is dissatisfied with what they have; no one believes they have *enough*. This sense—that no matter how much power and wealth we accumulate it isn't enough—forces us to look out only for ourselves, relinquishing our stewardship of the greater society.

Despite our problems, there's still a lot for us to feel good about. So why is there such a pervasive sense of dissatisfaction? The answer is that we're disconnected from the only thing that can satisfy us. We described it in Chapter 5, where it was called the Source—an all-giving power that created us, sustains us, and fills our future with endless possibilities. When we can't feel the Source as truly present in our lives, we feel alone and unsupported. It's those feelings that drive us to focus only on our narrow self-interest. Even those with power and privilege abandon their responsibility to the society at large.

A sense of stewardship can't be legislated. Laws and regulations might prevent the most egregious acts of irresponsibility, but they can't get inside of people and change the way they feel. Those in a position of authority will be moved to fulfill their responsibilities only when they feel grateful for how much they've been given. They must admit the truth: *no one reaches a position of authority without enormous amounts of help*—in the form of educational opportunity, unparalleled freedoms, or the fact that so many other individuals are willing to work in positions that are much less rewarding. Ultimately, this applies to all of us: when we appreciate everything we've been given, it will feel unnatural not to give back.

That's where the Grateful Flow comes in. In Chapter 5 you learned that gratefulness isn't just an emotion; it's actually the means by which you connect to the Source. When you use the Grateful Flow, you experience yourself as the beneficiary of its ceaseless generosity. The positive energy you generate inspires those around you to appreciate the blessings in their own lives. Only a wave of gratefulness sweeping across our whole society can counteract the degree of selfishness that's torn us apart.

Imagine what this would look like:

> Close your eyes and start ruminating on your dissatisfactions. Then, imagine the entire society around you in a similar, discontented state. How does this affect people's sense of responsibility for one another?
>
> Now, erase that image and do the Grateful Flow. Feel yourself overwhelmed with appreciativeness for everything you've been given from the day you were born. Now see millions of people around you using the tool and overflowing with gratefulness. How does this affect people's sense of responsibility for one another? How is the society you're envisioning now different from the one you started with?

Jeopardy

The four higher forces we've identified can reinvigorate the spirit of our society, but not if the individual members of that society won't do the work to bring those forces to bear. As a society, we're still waiting for a magical someone or something to make the changes happen without our effort. Nothing is more pathetic than knowing what needs to be done and not doing it. It's like watching someone die of a heart attack and waiting for someone else to initiate CPR.

What's dying isn't an individual. It's the spirit of our whole society. Never in our lifetimes has this been more obvious. We now know this, yet still we're paralyzed. Somehow, the danger doesn't seem quite real. Until it does, we can't find the willpower to act. That's where the Jeopardy tool comes in.

Each time you use Jeopardy, you break down your denial and activate your own will. But something more happens as well. The force of your willpower affects the people around you. It's as if one person starts doing CPR on the dying man. Suddenly awakened to what's at stake, another onlooker might call 911. Quickly, everyone around you is mobilized.

Let's go through your personal experience of Jeopardy and see its effect on the community around you. Before you start, pick out a typical situation where you should be using the tools but don't:

> Close your eyes and return to the image of the deathbed self you saw in Chapter 6. He sees your paralysis in the situation you picked and exhorts you not to waste the present moment, creating an urgent pressure to act. With your eyes still closed, relax for a moment and look around you. The willpower you've created has attracted a huge throng of others. Now use Jeopardy again but

> imagine the whole society using the tool with you.
> Feel the unstoppable power of its collective will.
> How does it change society?

This experience reveals why Jeopardy is the most crucial tool of all. We're a society made up of demoralized individuals. Each of us feels personally helpless to incite change. That makes it impossible for us to heal our spirit. But we have it wrong. The visualization you did a moment ago was more than an exercise for your benefit. The forces you felt have the power to save society. Don't wait for someone else to evoke them. No one is more qualified than you are.

NOW IT'S UP TO YOU

You're nearly at the end of the book. This is a crucial moment for you. What you do after you put this book down will dictate your future. If you wish to remain a consumer, you'll forget most of what you've read. Not only will you be untouched by the book, you also will have denied the importance of your own evolution—to yourself and to the world.

But if you aspire to be a creator, you're not finished.

To help you become a creator, the book has to do more than convey ideas; it has to awaken higher forces inside you. To keep those forces vital, you will have to use the tools long after you finish reading it—in fact, for the rest of your life. That's our ultimate goal: for you to maintain an unending relationship with higher forces. Call us crazy, but nothing less will satisfy us.

And if you aspire to be a creator, nothing less will satisfy you.

Throughout this book, we have tried to convey a simple but powerful truth: the power of higher forces is absolutely real. The longer they're a part of your life, the more profoundly they change you. By now we've had many patients who've lived with these forces for five, ten years or more. Their lives have become exceptional. Yes, many of them have enjoyed great success, but what's really exceptional is their response to failure. Constantly infused with higher forces, their spirit shines with a resiliency that's unstoppable.

When adversity comes, they welcome it, knowing that it will deepen their relationship with higher forces. Their reward is the ever-present support of something greater than themselves. This gives them an unshakeable confidence. They live bigger, fuller lives than they ever imagined they could—and they inspire others to do the same.

These people have the rarest of commodities: true happiness. Most of us never find it because we seek it in the outer world. Our ship never comes in because we're looking in the wrong place.

Real happiness is the constant presence of higher forces in our lives. And the universe has been designed so that higher forces are available every moment of every day. We simply have to use the tools to stay connected to them.

When enough people do this, the new spirituality will become more than an idea. It becomes a living organism whose fate depends on the efforts of individuals like you. This book is only an introduction to this process. The new spirituality requires you to go beyond the book, asking your own questions and discovering new answers about the human spirit. Doing this doesn't just benefit you; the new spirituality dies without it. The future is your responsibility.

We did not write this book for consumers to digest and eliminate like fast food. Nor did we write it to enlist adherents or followers. We wrote it so that you, as a creator, would move the new spirituality forward in your own unique way, no matter what your circumstances are. If you do, though we may never meet, we will be connected forever.

ACKNOWLEDGMENTS

First, I want to thank my co-author and friend Barry Michels. His drive got this project going, his faith kept it going during the darkest moments. He treated my ideas with loving care but constantly went beyond them in ways I never could have. He's a rare combination of fairness, sensitivity, and passion. I would trust him with my life.

I also want to thank Joel Simon, my lifelong friend, who is no longer with us. He taught me what courage really is.

Lastly, I want to acknowledge the group of friends and colleagues who were generous enough to read the book as a work in progress. I particularly valued their input because they were already familiar with the tools and concepts I was struggling to describe. Each of the following individuals made a crucial contribution: Michael Bygrave, Nancy Dunn, Vanessa Inn, Barbara McNally, Sharon O'Connor, and Maria Semple.

Phil Stutz

Foremost among the people I want to thank are my co-author and friend, Phil Stutz, and my wife, Judy White. I could not have written this book without both. Phil is quite simply the most uniquely gifted individual I've ever met. His wisdom penetrates so deeply into the essence of things that I cannot think of a single question of mine he failed to answer—and his answers were always startlingly incisive, yet delivered with tremendous passion and warmth. Likewise, it is impossible to give adequate thanks to my wife. She has been unfailingly loyal and supportive and I love her with all my heart.

I also want to thank my (adult) children, Hana and Jesse. Their support—from specific edits to more general love and goodwill—means the world to me. Jesse took a particular interest in the wider, societal impact of the tools and was a big factor in our decision to include it in the book.

So many friends—Jane Garnett, Vanessa Inn, Steve Kivelson, Steve Motenko, and Allison and David White—encouraged me with their warmth and unshakable support. Thank you for expressing confidence in me when I lost all confidence in myself.

Finally, I would like to thank my patients. Every day I feel honored and deeply humbled that you entrust yourselves to me. The connections I feel with you are among the closest I've forged with anyone. Thank you for sharing the deepest parts of yourselves with me. And thank you for the very tangible help you've given me in bringing this book to fruition.

Barry Michels

We both want to thank Yvonne Wish for helping with the myriad details related to the book. Her diligence, foresight, and attention to detail saved us innumerable times.

We also thank Michael Gendler and Jason Sloane for taking us through the complex negotiation process with grace and fairness for all. Without their perspective and experience we would have needed therapy ourselves.

Random House has been incredibly generous with its time and resources, a wonderful home for our book. Our editor, Julie Grau, is one of the greatest—she is astute yet flexible, and we felt she "got" our material immediately. Theresa Zoro and Sanyu Dillon, as well as their entire staffs, were amazingly supportive in giving us feedback and helping us along on the journey.

We'd also like to thank our agent, Jennifer Rudolf Walsh. From day one we knew we'd found a soulmate. She immediately understood what we were about, what our goals and values were, and set about championing our work with indefatigable energy and inexhaustible skill.

Finally we never would have met Julie Grau or Jennifer Walsh if a supremely talented journalist, Dana Goodyear, hadn't decided to write about our work in *The New Yorker*. She did this with a level of care and respect for which we'll be forever grateful.

Phil Stutz and Barry Michels

About the Authors

PHIL STUTZ graduated from City College in New York and received his MD from New York University. He worked as a prison psychiatrist on Rikers Island and then in private practice in New York before moving his practice to Los Angeles in 1982.

BARRY MICHELS has a BA from Harvard, a law degree from University of California, Berkeley, and an MSW from the University of Southern California. He has been in private practice as a psychotherapist since 1986.